# Contents

# About this book

**C**ongratulations on your decision to take Edexcel's Foundation Diploma in Information Technology! This book will help you with all six units of your course, providing opportunities to develop functional skills, Personal, Learning and Thinking Skills, and to learn about the world of work.

There is a chapter devoted to every unit, and each chapter opens with the following:

» Overview – a description of what is covered in the unit

» Skills list – a checklist of the skills covered in the unit

» Job watch – a list of relevant careers

This book contains many features that will help you relate your learning to the workplace and assist you in making links to other parts of the Diploma.

» Margin notes provide interesting facts and get you thinking about the industry.

**FIND OUT**
See if you can find out what services ATMs offer in addition to taking out money from the customer's account.

**DID YOU KNOW?**
Personal information about a bank account or a PIN is confidential. These details should not be given to anyone who phones or emails asking for them – even if they say they are from the bank.

**TRY THIS**
If you have never tried an on-screen test before, log onto the following website and try a Level 1 Literacy (English) or Numeracy (Maths) test.
www1.edexcel.org.uk/tot/alns2/CMA-Edexcel-web2.2.swf

**CHECK IT OUT**
Visit www.btbroadband inforamtion.com and click on the 'Glossary' tab. You will find many useful definitions there, including Cat 5, Ethernet cable, hub, optical cable and Wi-Fi.

» Activities link directly to Personal, Learning and Thinking Skills and functional skills – all an important part of passing your course and vital for your future career.

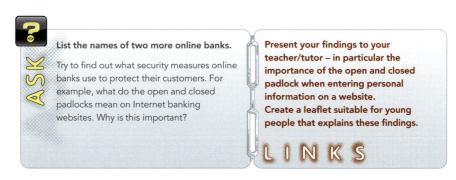

**ASK**
List the names of two more online banks.

Try to find out what security measures online banks use to protect their customers. For example, what do the open and closed padlocks mean on Internet banking websites. Why is this important?

Present your findings to your teacher/tutor – in particular the importance of the open and closed padlock when entering personal information on a website.
Create a leaflet suitable for young people that explains these findings.

**LINKS**

**»** @work activities help you to think about how your learning could be applied during your work placement.

When you are on your work experience, take time to observe your colleagues. Identify **one** thing about each of your colleagues that you think is a good example of their professionalism.

At the end of your work experience, ask your manager to identify **three** things about your behaviour at work that were professional behaviours.

**»** A Case Study feature provides a snapshot of real issues in the workplace.

**»** 'I want to be a…' provides an snapshot of real people working in Information Technology.

Each chapter ends with assessment tips and an opportunity for you to check your skills and summarise what you've learned. You can also find help with technical terms in the glossary on page 204.

We hope you enjoy using this book, and we wish you the very best for your Diploma course and your future career in Information Technology.

# OVERVIEW

We increasingly use computers and computer devices to do things such as record keeping, trading and communicating, that we would previously have done manually. These technologies can impact significantly on the way in which businesses operate. They may be used to support a wide variety of business activities and have the power to improve efficiency, open up new markets and enhance customer service.

This unit looks at some of the technology systems used by businesses. For example, the way in which consumers shop has been changed by automated teller machines (ATMs), Electronic Point of Sale (EPOS) and the many online and telephone facilities for banking and shopping.

Understanding the basic components of systems and being able to identify the role of a variety of devices is essential. This unit discusses the key components of technology systems = the hardware, software, communications and networks.

Businesses need to review their technological needs frequently, due to rapid technological developments and the changing needs of the organisation. A business can become more successful when it implements a new technology system or improves its current systems. This unit helps you to recognise when a business might benefit from a new or improved system.

# Technology in Organisations

# Know the key components of technology systems used in business

## What is a technology system?

A technology system is a collection of electronic devices and programs that are put together in a particular way (configured) to do a specific job or activity. Over the years, technology systems have been modified in different ways to meet the needs of different types of organisation. Some examples of this follow.

## Banking

Banking systems have benefited enormously from the introduction of technology in areas such as processing cheques for payment, and allowing customers remote access to money from their personal account. The following are some examples of the technologies available to customers.

### Automated teller machines (ATMs)

The first ATMs were found inside banks and building society branches. They could be used only when these organisations were open for business. Today, as well as being found outside premises, ATMs are commonly found in supermarkets, petrol stations, airports, railway stations and many, many more places. They are usually available for use 24-hours a day.

To use an ATM you need a bank or building society card and a PIN (Personal Identification Number) which is unique and known only by the card holder.

Users insert the card into the machine and key in their PIN. Once they have done this, they can choose from a series of options. At the end of the transaction (business), the machine returns the card to the user.

### Home banking

Using home banking technology, banks can offer services to customers from the comfort of their own homes. Home banking consists of telephone banking and online banking.

**FIGURE 1.1**
**Cashpoint machine**

**DID YOU KNOW?**

Transaction is the word for any business carried out. For example, if cash is withdrawn from an ATM or an account balance is checked, these are transactions. Other transactions may include buying something from a shop; paying for a meal in a restaurant.

**FIND OUT**

See if you can find out what services ATMs offer in addition to taking out money from the customer's account.

### Telephone banking

Telephone banking allows the customer to carry out transactions using a digital telephone keypad to enter numbers when prompted by a recorded message. The customer also has the option of talking to an operator. Using a computer and with the customer's permission, the operator can access the customer's account while talking to them on the telephone and carry out the transactions requested.

### Online banking

Online banking is when the user can access their account via the Internet. Most high street banks such as Barclays™, Lloyds TSB™ and NatWest™ have online banking facilities. However, there are some banks that operate only online: for example, smile.co.uk is an Internet-only bank with no High Street branches.

**ASK**

**List the names of two more online banks.**

Try to find out what security measures online banks use to protect their customers. For example, what do the open and closed padlocks mean on Internet banking websites. Why is this important?

**Present your findings to your teacher/tutor – in particular the importance of the open and closed padlock when entering personal information on a website.**
**Create a leaflet suitable for young people that explains these findings.**

**L I N K S**

## Retail

A retailer is any organisation that sells products direct to the public, such as shops and restaurants. Much of the technology used by these organisations will be very familiar to you.

### Electronic Point of Sale (EPOS)

EPOS is the system used to adjust stock and take payments as items are sold in shops. Each item has a barcode. When a customer wants to pay for the item selected, the item's barcode is scanned at the store's checkout point (till). The information picked up by this scan is relayed to a central stock system that automatically reduces the stock total by one item. Once the sale is complete, the amount the customer has paid is automatically logged in the store's records.

FIGURE 1.2 **Scanning at a supermarket checkout**

Before computers, staff in shops had to go to the shelves, or racks, and count how many items were on them. They then had to take that number away from the number of items that were originally put out. The difference was the number they had sold. With EPOS, staff no longer have to check the shelves because the sales are scanned through the till or checkout system and automatically taken off the stock total.

Using EPOS also means that shops have much more information about customers. For example, they know:

» which products are, or are not, selling well

» whether products sell better on one day rather than on another

» if the position of a product on a shelf makes a difference to whether customers buy it.

This information is used to decide how to purchase (buy) stock. Buying stock more carefully saves retailers money as, for example, fewer goods have to be thrown away or sold at a reduced price because they are near to their sell-by date.

### Electronic Funds Transfer at Point of Sale (EFTPOS)

An EFTPOS device allows the retailer to receive payment directly from the customer's bank when the customer uses their bank card to pay. The card is inserted into the retailer's card reader and the customer keys in their PIN. The money is withdrawn immediately from their bank account and paid to the shop.

FIGURE 1.3
Supermarket checkout card reader

### Loyalty cards

A loyalty card is issued by a shop (usually one that is part of a large chain of shops such as one of the major supermarkets) in exchange for the customer's personal information. The customer then presents the card each time they make a purchase and receives points, which are recorded against their personal account.

When the customer has earned enough points, they receive some sort of reward from the store. This could be in the form of money-off vouchers, discounts or in some cases free products.

The introduction of loyalty cards has various advantages to shops and other organisations that issue them.

For example, it means that:

FIGURE 1.4
Loyalty cards

» customers will choose to shop with a particular organisation to build up points which they can exchange for goods or vouchers

» the data collected when the card is used enables the organisation to build a profile of customers such as their age group and what products they buy

» comparisons of differences in buying patterns can be made between people of the same age who live in different parts of the country

» decisions about which products to stock, which to develop and which to delete from a range can be made more easily

» profits improve because the organisation no longer stocks products that they cannot sell and they can also make sure they do not run out of stock of products that sell well.

### Self-service checkouts

FIGURE 1.5 **Self-service checkout**

Many supermarkets have introduced self-service checkouts where customers can scan their purchases and pay without the help of a shop assistant.

### Food purchases

MacDonalds™ and Brewers Fayre™ are examples of food outlets that offer customers a fast service. Therefore, they have introduced systems that allow staff to enter and store food orders, then process payment once orders are complete. Touch sensitive screens are used, making the process both easier and faster for staff to use. These screens are common in many retail organisations.

FIGURE 1.6
Touch sensitive till

## E-commerce

E-commerce is the general term used for companies trading online. It is a shorter way of saying electronic trading. The 'e' is for electronic and 'commerce' means trading.

The following are some examples of how technology is used in online trading.

### Online auction sites

These websites are used by both businesses and the general public to buy and sell new and used items. The range of items you can buy on such sites is huge. eBay™ is an example of an online auction site.

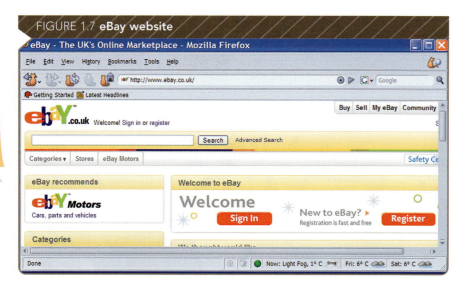

FIGURE 1.7 eBay website

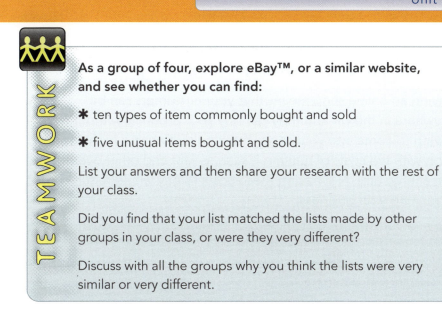

**TEAMWORK**

As a group of four, explore eBay™, or a similar website, and see whether you can find:

✱ ten types of item commonly bought and sold

✱ five unusual items bought and sold.

List your answers and then share your research with the rest of your class.

Did you find that your list matched the lists made by other groups in your class, or were they very different?

Discuss with all the groups why you think the lists were very similar or very different.

**LINKS**

Plan your research and keep a copy of your research plan in your portfolio.

Create a PowerPoint presentation to introduce the subject of online auction sites to the rest of your class.

## Music downloads

Many people feel that the days of buying CDs are coming to an end as both individual tracks and whole CDs can be downloaded from websites such as Apple iTunes and Napster. These sites are easy to use. For example, accessing the Napster shop is easy and the user simply clicks to download the tracks that they want. The items downloaded are totalled and an invoice sent to the user who pays using an online payment service.

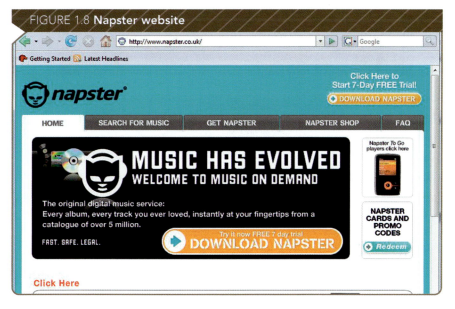

FIGURE 1.8 Napster website

## Internet shopping

The easiest way to think about online shopping is to imagine that you own a high-street shop. Customers can come into your shop and look around. They can buy some of your products and, if they are happy with your service and products, they will hopefully come back and buy more at a later date. If everyone in the country could come into your shop, you'd be able to sell more products.

Having an online shop means that your customers can be anywhere in the UK and they can buy your products without ever having to come into your shop. You wouldn't need a high-street shop with the costs of running it such as rent and other overheads like energy bills. Not having these costs to pay would reduce costs of running your business.

FIGURE 1.9 German online supermarket

It doesn't stop there. Not only can you actually sell to everyone in the UK, you can also sell your goods anywhere in the world (providing you remember to charge the customer extra for postage), so effectively you reach a much wider market than if you have a high-street shop. Organisations around the world can also sell to you, which might allow you to increase the range of products offered. It might also allow you to buy them at a cheaper price.

Also, you effectively have longer opening hours because a customer can buy products at any time of the day or night. Your business can be open 24 hours a day, 7 days a week.

The disadvantage of buying goods over the Internet is that customers have to wait for the goods to arrive by post or parcel service. If the items are needed urgently, the customer has to pay higher delivery charges to take advantage, for example, of next-day delivery services.

## Payment systems (services)

There are a number of possible payment systems. These include EFTPOS, which was described earlier. However, online traders are more likely to use an electronic payment system (also known as a payment service).

The most commonly used payment services are:

» PayPal

» NoChex.

The systems provide a secure service that transfers money between the customer (buyer) and the supplier (seller). This type of service is usually quick and reliable and gives customers a level of security.

**FIND OUT**

Visit www.paypal.co.uk and find out what personal services and products and services are available.

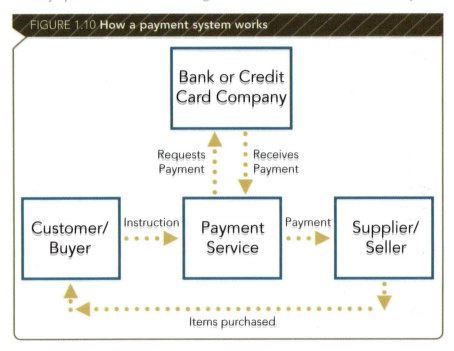

FIGURE 1.10 **How a payment system works**

This is how it works:

» The customer tells the payment service to make the payment for the items purchased to the supplier or seller.

» The payment service checks with the customer's bank or credit-card company that the customer's account has enough money to pay for the items.

» The payment service receives payment from the customer's bank or credit-card company, which is then passed to the seller's account.

» The items purchased can then be sent to the customer.

When described, this seems like a long-winded process. However, as it is done electronically, it is more or less instant.

## Sport and leisure

### *Performance monitoring of individuals within a sports centre*
Personal trainers are using technology increasingly to monitor individual performance. Some equipment has a digital display to show information about how the person exercising is performing – for example, how many strokes per minute the person is achieving (as shown in Figure 1.11). Some displays also give readouts for heart rate.

FIGURE 1.11 **Electronic data display**

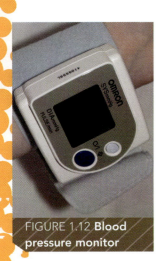
FIGURE 1.12 **Blood pressure monitor**

Technology also allows individuals to monitor their own performance. For example, devices such as a blood pressure monitor can be worn on the wrist so that the person exercising can see how their blood pressure readings change with exercise.

### *Attendance monitoring*
Another example of technology used by sports organisations is the database used to store records about a centre or club membership. Figure 1.13 shows that a photograph has been included to prevent someone other than the member from gaining access to the premises.

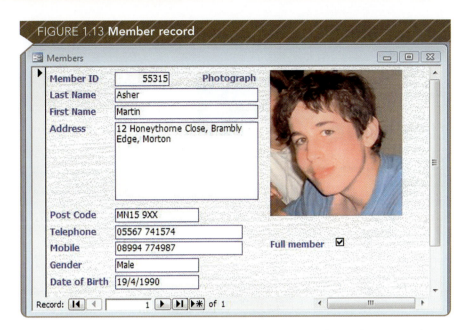

FIGURE 1.13 **Member record**

**FIND OUT**

Talk to your friends and family and find out whether any of them have photo ID cards.

The system also stores booking information such as the court the member has reserved, and the date and time of the activity.

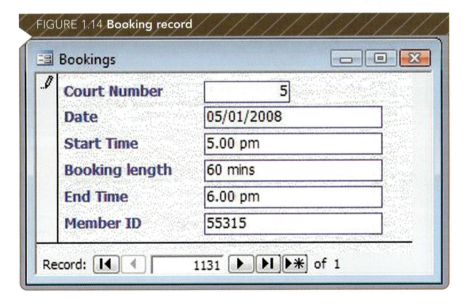

FIGURE 1.14 **Booking record**

*Buying/reserving cinema tickets*

Cinema and theatre tickets can be easily reserved or bought online. The customer chooses the film they would like to see, the date they want to see it and the location of the cinema – most of these choices are made from a dropdown menu (a series of boxes that appear on the screen as choices are entered).

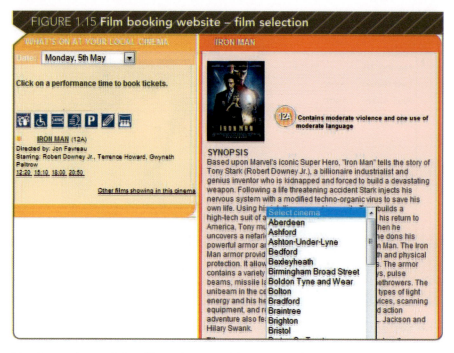

FIGURE 1.15 **Film booking website – film selection**

Having selected the film, date and location, the customer uses the dropdown menu to select the number of tickets, remembering to choose whether they are adults or children as this affects the price paid.

FIGURE 1.16 **Film booking website – ticket choice**

Once the booking is confirmed, the customer is asked to provide their personal details. The customer is required to give a valid email address so that confirmation can be sent to them.

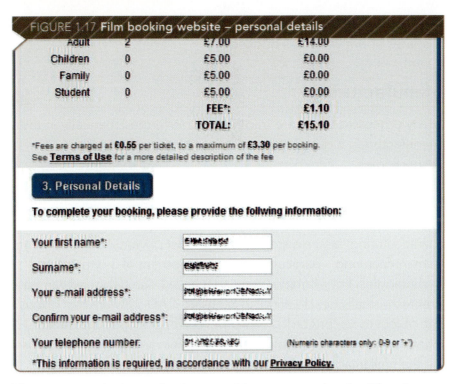

FIGURE 1.17 Film booking website – personal details

The customer is then asked to provide payment details. (The cinema often charges an additional fee for using the online service.)

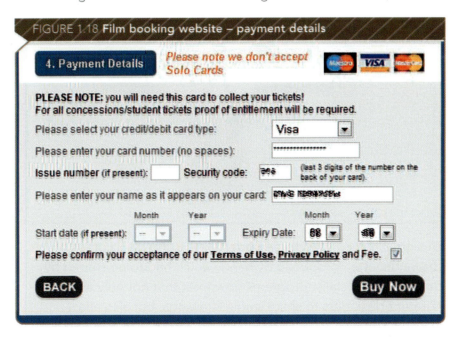

FIGURE 1.18 Film booking website – payment details

The booking is confirmed and the customer can print out the confirmation. An email confirmation will also be sent.

Usually, the customer then collects the tickets from the cinema by presenting the card they used to make the online payment. However, it is always useful for the customer to take a copy of the email or the web confirmation with them in case there are any disputes about what was booked.

## Manufacturing

Many processes that were traditionally performed manually in the manufacturing industry are now done using a variety of technologies.

### CAD/CAM

CAD (computer-aided design) and CAM (computer-aided manufacturing) systems are two of the most powerful developments in manufacturing – particularly the development of 3-dimensional technologies. For example, items that have been designed can be created virtually (real looking) in 3D using CAD software that allows the object to be 'printed' on a 3D printer. In principle, the item is printed through the combination of powders and glues. These build up the final image layer by layer. Other developments include product and component modelling for engineering.

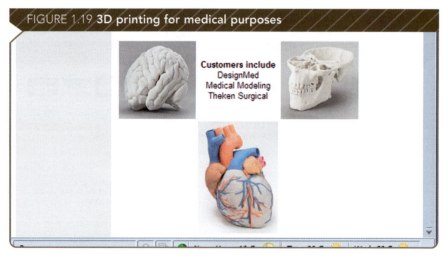

FIGURE 1.19 **3D printing for medical purposes**

Customers include
DesignMed
Medical Modeling
Theken Surgical

Design activities used to be undertaken using hard copies of drawings, often produced by hand, which had to be shared by designers. Specialist programs now exist that not only allow different designers to share single drawings, but also allow multiple users to work on the same drawing at the same time.

The advantages of using CAD/CAM include:

» drawings can be updated easily

» drawings are stored electronically (so they don't take up a lot of physical file space)

» additional electronic copies of drawings can be made for security (in case the original is lost or damaged).

The disadvantages of using CAD/CAM include:

» keeping track of different versions of diagrams

» diagrams that are not easy to update still need to be redrawn.

### Process control

Manufacturing organisations make things that they sell to other businesses or to individuals directly as partly or completely finished products. They buy raw materials and turn them into finished goods. This includes products such as food, clothing, furniture, paper products, chemicals, metal and electronic components.

Do you know anyone who works with systems that are controlled by computers?

FIGURE 1.20 **Robotic car manufacturing**

Some entire manufacturing processes are now fully automated and controlled by computer technology. One of the best known examples is the car manufacturing process, where robots build and process most of the car infrastructure with minimal human input.

FIGURE 1.21 **Packing beauty products**

Some companies have automated packaging processes that use computer-operated packing machines capable of packing a wide range of products, including perishable and easily damaged products like fruit or vegetables.

## Transport and logistics

### *Global positioning systems (GPS)*

GPS allows users to know exactly where they are and also to find the best route between two or more locations. It works by converting signals from satellites in space into user-friendly location maps that can be displayed on computerised receivers inside vehicles. This is particularly useful for the emergency services such as police, fire engine and ambulance drivers who previously had to have extensive local knowledge.

**FIND OUT**

Talk to your friends and family and find out whether anyone relies on GPS technology to help them in their job.

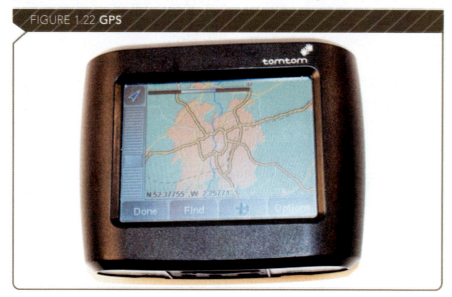

FIGURE 1.22 **GPS**

The advantages of using GPS is that:

» it is a portable device containing maps and POIs (points of interest)

» its main component is a touch-operated display screen

» it uses satellites to pinpoint an exact position

» it can be used by anyone travelling by road, sea or air

» it can improve the efficiency of the emergency services

» delivery drivers, for example, don't have to rely on local knowledge or map reading when going to new locations.

## Traffic control

Almost all traffic control systems make use of technology, from simple traffic light systems to air traffic control systems. Air traffic control systems are often complex systems that display large quantities of information at the same time. The air traffic controller's job is to interpret this information and use it to coordinate air traffic movements, making sure that all aircraft are safe in the air.

FIGURE 1.23 **Air traffic control**

## Route finders

FIGURE 1.24 **AA Route planner**

Like GPS, a route finder uses Internet technology to find the best route between locations. The user can make a printout of the route to take with them on their journey.

Websites such as www.theaa.com allow users to choose the level of detail that they need. Figure 1.24 shows that information about petrol stations, speed cameras and traffic black spots, for example, can be included.

**FIND OUT**

See if you can find your way from your house to your school or college using a route planner such as www.theaa.com or www.rac.co.uk.

Tip: It is much easier if you use the post codes from each address.

FIGURE 1.25 **AA Route plan**

| Travel (miles) | and then | to take | show map | total (miles) |
|---|---|---|---|---|
| 0.00 | Start out at BS1, Bristol | A420 | | 0.00 |
| 0.10 | At Lawrence Hill roundabout take the 1st exit onto the A4320 | A4320 | | 0.10 |
| 0.54 | At roundabout take the 3rd exit onto the A4320 (signposted London, South Wales) | A4320 | | 0.64 |
| 0.22 | Continue forward, then join the M32 motorway (signposted Stapleton, Frenchay, M32) | M32 | | 0.86 |
| 0.74 | Bristol - Jct 2 | M32 | | 1.60 |
| 3.39 | At roundabout take the 2nd exit, then join the M4 motorway (signposted London) | M4 | | 4.98 |
| 16.19 | Leigh Delamere Service Area | M4 | | 21.17 |
| 28.14 | Membury Service Area | M4 | | 49.32 |
| 11.34 | Chieveley Service Area | M4 | | 60.65 |
| 13.77 | Reading Service Area | M4 | | 74.42 |

## Number plate recognition

In some cities, for example London, there is a central London Congestion Charge. Vehicles liable to pay the daily charge are detected via the use of CCTV technology and using automatic number plate recognition software. Payments can be made online.

FIGURE 1.26 **Congestion charging website**

## Item tracking

Some distribution companies are making use of GPS tracking technology to track packages from the moment they leave the company to the point when they arrive with the customer. Many of these organisations offer customers the opportunity to track the progress of their package online, using a tracking number allocated to their package.

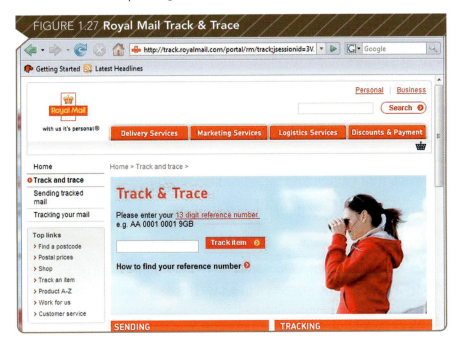

FIGURE 1.27 **Royal Mail Track & Trace**

# Key components of technology systems

As suggested previously, technology systems are made up of a series of components or devices that are configured for a particular purpose. This section investigates the types of components that make up most systems.

## Personal computers (PCs or workstations)

These are the commonest type of computer in use. They are made up of a monitor, a base unit, keyboard and mouse and can be attached to a network. Workstations are static – they are meant to stay in one place.

## Laptops

Laptops are portable computers that can be taken from place to place. They are made up of a monitor, a base unit, keyboard and mouse, combined into a single unit. Laptops are small and lightweight - usually the size of a thick folder. They can be carried

FIGURE 1.28
**Personal computer**

FIGURE 1.29
**Laptop PC**

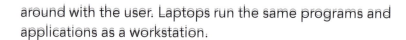

around with the user. Laptops run the same programs and applications as a workstation.

### Servers

Servers are often stored away from the main workstations in designated cabinets. A server is a bit like a master computer that manages a specific resource or set of resources (such as a network). Some systems have a range of servers each of which will have a specific function:

» **print servers** manage printers and make sure that the resources are used efficiently

» **email servers** look after an organisation's email traffic (incoming, outgoing and within the organisation)

» **file servers** are often a computer attached to a master storage device that handle and organise file storage.

» **network servers** control network traffic.

**FIGURE 1.30**
**Server rack**

### Mainframe

A mainframe is a computer capable of processing large quantities of information. They are often used by big companies and serve large numbers of users.

**FIGURE 1.31**
**Mainframe**

## Input devices

An input device enables a user to interact with a system, to give instructions to the system by clicking on buttons or keying in commands. They also allow users to input data that will be stored or manipulated by the system. You will be familiar with input devices such as a computer keyboard and a mouse. However, the range of technologies is growing.

### Touch screen

More and more devices now use touch screen technology. One of the first examples of this technology was the personal digital assistant (PDA).

PDAs are hand-held devices that run versions of standard programs with limited functionality. They are touch-operated using a stylus (or you can use your finger). Figure 1.32 shows an example of a PDA.

**FIGURE 1.32**
**PDA**

# Optical Mark Reader/Recognition (OMR)

OMRs scan pre-printed forms looking for the position of marks that have been placed on the form with a pen or pencil to indicate a selection or choice. A lottery ticket form is an example of an OMR used for data input. The form contains a series of small rectangles which the user marks with a block or line to show their choices.

It looks something like the following.

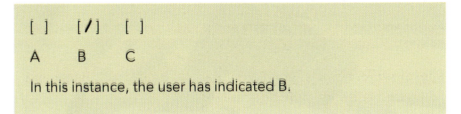

```
[ ]    [/]    [ ]

A      B      C
```

In this instance, the user has indicated B.

**FIGURE 1.33**
**Lottery form**

Using OMR forms has several advantages, for example:

» it is easy to collect information

» they don't require much training to use

» they are often used for multiple-choice questionnaires or exams.

Some disadvantages of using OMR forms are that:

» forms can be easily damaged if creased or folded and incorrect information will be put into the system

» errors will occur if they are not correctly filled in (for example, using the wrong colour pen)

» they have limited uses.

## Optical Character Reader/Recognition OCR

OCR devices also read paper documents, but use scanning technology and specialist software to convert the document text into ASCII characters that can then be worked with and/or stored in a system. One of the most recent uses of this technology is scanning passport information when individuals enter or leave a country.

**FIGURE 1.34**
**Passport reader**

**DID YOU KNOW?**

ASCII is short for the American Standard Code for Information Interchange. It is a method of electronically coding computer text that was developed from the telegraphic code.

## Bar code scanner

A bar code is a series of vertical lines on a label that can be scanned by a bar code reader or scanner. Each line represents a different number. The combined number can identify an item such as a book, a DVD or an item of food in a supermarket.

The scanner reads the number, interprets it and the computer program looks up the number in a file to find the relevant information.

## Biometric scanner

FIGURE 1.37 **A fingerprint scanner**

Biometric scanners use the physical features or attributes of the human body to provide unique information about an individual. They are commonly used for locks that give access to premises or systems and use information that has been scanned and stored in a database. When the user wishes to gain access to the premises or system, he or she allows the same physical feature to be scanned and the system compares the scan with the version held on record. If there is a complete match, the access is granted.

FIGURE 1.35
**A bar code**

FIGURE 1.36
**A bar code reader**

ASK

**Use the Internet to investigate the different features of the body that can be used to provide useful biometric data.**

Make a plan of how you intend to use the Internet and keep a list of the websites you visit.

Identify at least five features and what types of organisation might use these types of scan.

**Keep the plan in your portfolio, making sure that you have listed your sources.**

LINKS

### Magnetic stripe reader
Plastic cards that fit into your wallet or purse often contain magnetic stripes that hold information digitally. Some common examples include bank cards, credit cards, shop loyalty cards, library cards and travel passes.

A more recent application of this technology is for hotel door keys. These keys are no longer of the metal variety, but are plastic cards that are pushed into a slot in the door handle. A red light means that the door is locked. A green one, that the lock has been opened.

These types of card are popular because they are:

» inexpensive

» easy to use

» quick

» not damaged easily.

In the event that a customer accidentally takes or loses a key card, the lock number can be simply changed (in fact, it is usual to change it for each new customer).However, these cards are very easy to copy and the data on the stripe can be easily corrupted if exposed to magnets.

### Chip and PIN

In recent years, chip and PIN technology has replaced magnetic stripes on bank and credit cards. Present day cards contain a computer microchip (Figure 1.40) that holds information about the account holder.

When the customer is ready to pay for goods or services, they simply insert their payment card into the card reader and key in their PIN. After the transaction is complete, the customer and the store both keep a paper printout of the details.

FIGURE 1.38
**Hotel door lock**

FIGURE 1.39 **Magnetic stripe on a card**

FIGURE 1.40
**Chip on a bank card**

JOIN IN

**With a group of classmates, find out about chip and PIN using the following website:**

http://www.chipandpin.co.uk/

Answer the following questions:

✱ What if someone has seen your PIN?

✱ What if I forget my PIN?

✱ What does it mean if my card is locked?

**Create an A4 leaflet that explains chip and PIN technology.**

**Make sure it includes advice on what to do if you think security has been compromised (for example, someone has seen or copied your PIN).**

LINKS

**FIGURE 1.41**
**A movement sensor**

### Sensors

Sensors are usually attached to devices. The sensor measures a factor such as movement, heat or light and sends the information back to the device. The device contains a computer program that monitors the information sent by the sensor and reacts to this depending on its programming. For example, sensors can detect when someone enters a room and send a signal to a device to turn on the lights.

The sensor in Figure 1.41 is attached to a security system. When the light is lit (usually red) it has sensed movement.

## Output devices

The outputs from a computer usually come in a visual form (one that you can see), an audio form (one that you can hear) or a physical form, such as a document (one that you can touch). The following are some common examples.

**FIGURE 1.42**
**A CRT monitor**

### Monitor

The monitor is used to display the video image generated by the graphics card inside the computer.

Older monitors use bulky CRT (Cathode Ray Tube) technology.

Newer monitors are slimmer, flat panel LCDs (Liquid Crystal Display).

You may remember from earlier in this unit that some monitors can also have touch sensitive screens.

**FIGURE 1.43**
**An LCD monitor**

### Printer

Along with monitors, printers are the most commonly used output device. They create hard copies (paper versions) of the images you see on screen.

FIGURE 1.44 **A printer**

**FIND OUT**

There are various types of printer on the market today. See if you can identify three different types.

It is likely that you will have access to more than one type of printer in your school or at home.

### Plotter

Plotters are not dissimilar to printers. They have a paper output; however, plotters use a mechanism that moves over the surface of the paper and draws on it using a range of coloured inks. These devices are usually capable of creating outputs on large and very large paper (A3 size and above) and are often used in engineering to output complex drawings. They can be used to create paper patterns for clothing or maps of the ocean floor.

### Data projector

The data projector is often used with a second device known as an interactive whiteboard. The projector (Figure 1.45) beams the image onto the whiteboard (Figure 1.46) and special software allows the user to turn pages, write on the image, to highlight aspects of the image and so on. This technology is rapidly replacing the traditional board that used marker pens.

FIGURE 1.45
A data projector

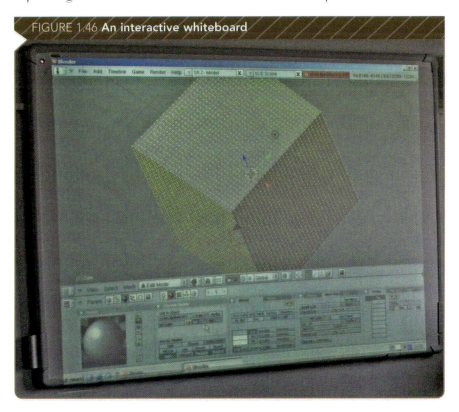
FIGURE 1.46 **An interactive whiteboard**

### Speakers

Speakers convert computer outputs into sound. The level of sound (volume) can be adjusted to suit the user.

FIGURE 1.47
Speakers

### Control devices

Automated manufacturing relies on the output of systems to control the manufacturing process. What was originally done by people (such as switching machines on and off, or changing settings) can now be undertaken by a computer. The main advantage of using control devices is that they require less human input, so fewer workers are needed. In turn, this means that production costs can be reduced.

### Storage devices

Storage devices include anything that can store and carry information between computers. Some examples follow.

### Hard disks

FIGURE 1.48
**Hard disk**

The hard disk is used to store both the software and data in an IT system. The hard disk is not usually removed (unless it needs to be replaced). The hard disk may store anything between 10 and 350 Gigabytes.

### Portable media such as CDs and DVDs

FIGURE 1.49
**DVD drive**

CDs and DVDs come in two varieties, single-use disks that are writeable (can be written to only once) and multiple-use disks that are re-writeable (can be written to more than once). The disks must be inserted in a CD or DVD drive.

A drive is a device used to read a compact disc (CD) or digital versatile disc (DVD). Some devices can write data to blank CDs and/or DVDs. These are often called CD/DVD 'burners'.

### USB sticks

FIGURE 1.50 **USB stick/Flash drive**

In recent years, computers are more likely to be sold with USB reading devices than with floppy disk drives. Current USB flash drives have a large memory capacity and are becoming cheaper to produce.

A 4GB flash drive like the one shown in Figure 1.50 is capable of storing about the same amount of data and images as 40 floppy disks.

### Floppy disks

FIGURE 1.51
**Floppy disk**

Before the arrival of USB storage devices, most computers had floppy disk drives. These disks had only a small storage capacity (up to 1.44 megabytes of data).

To read from the disks and write to them, they had to be inserted into a floppy disk drive. The one shown in Fig 1.52 is an external floppy drive that can be connected to a computer through a USB connection or port.

## Communication

FIGURE 1.52
**External floppy drive**

This section covers communications between devices.

### Networking (wired and wireless)

Networks fall into one of two categories – wired and wireless:

» wired network devices are connected by Ethernet cables

» wireless networks are connected by wireless radio waves. A device like the wireless dongle shown in Figure 1.54 is attached to each end of the connection.

Wireless devices are popular but they are less secure than wired devices, and signals can be weakened by distance and interference.

FIGURE 1.53
**Ethernet cable**

### Mobile devices

Communication on the move can be achieved through two common devices – the mobile phone and the Blackberry™.

Mobile phones:

» are portable communication devices

» are made up of a keypad, a screen, a microphone and a speaker

» can be connected to the Internet

» may have camera options

» may play MP3s.

FIGURE 1.54 **Wireless Internet dongle**

The primary use of the Blackberry is to send and receive emails, although it also supports text messaging, Internet browsing and can be used as a mobile phone.

Much like mobile phones, these devices function wherever they can receive a wireless signal. They allow an individual on the move to stay in direct contact with customers, suppliers and their office.

FIGURE 1.56
**Blackberry**

FIGURE 1.55
**Mobile phone**

## Software

### *Operating system software*

The operating system is the master program that controls the workings of the computer. An application like Microsoft Office cannot be directly loaded onto a computer without an operating system. Without an operating system, a computer is just a box of nuts, bolts and electronic circuits!

### *Applications software*

This is the general term for applications or programs that are developed and designed to carry out specific tasks.

FIGURE 1.57 Microsoft Office Suite

Examples include:

» spreadsheets

» databases

» planning software

» word processing

» presentation software

» Internet browsers.

## Communication software

Communication software includes applications such as email and instant messaging.

Instant messaging software allows users to talk in text in real time. This means that people can effectively talk in real time by each person typing in their part of the conversation.

## Security software

It is absolutely essential that systems are as secure as possible against potential threats from hackers, spyware and computer viruses. New spyware and viruses are being written daily, so both software components must be updated regularly. The following are some examples of common security software.

### Anti-virus

This is a software component that will detect, repair or delete files that have been infected with a computer virus. Some anti-virus software can be downloaded free.

FIGURE 1.58
**Instant Messaging**

FIGURE 1.59 **Some free anti-virus software**

### Anti-spyware

Spyware can be accidentally installed onto an IT system where it can track downloads, websites visited and record the user's keystrokes. Anti-spyware is a software component that can detect and remove spyware.

### Firewall

A firewall is either a hardware or software component that filters network traffic. The firewall's job is to spot bad network data or unauthorised network activity. Firewalls are usually set to check network data coming into and going out from an organisation's network.

# Know why an organisation should implement or improve a technology system

**B**efore iTunes and Napster, there were music CDs. Before music CDs, there were records pressed out of plastic and played with a stylus. We all accept that at times things wear out or become outdated and we need to replace them. When it comes to implementing technology or improving an existing system, organisations need to weigh up the pros and cons carefully.

## Why might an organisation implement a system or improve an existing one?

The following are some reasons why organisations might improve or implement systems:

» To improve the performance of their current system – for example, because the existing system has become slow (it takes a long time to load programs and open or save files).

» To cut their costs – investing in technology could reduce their need for people.

» To take advantage of better technologies – because the organisation needs to load software that is not compatible with other aspects of the system. Each software application has a minimum requirement specification that is needed to allow the software to run correctly and this may not be met by the existing system.

» To access new markets – for example, online trading.

» Because larger storage options are required – more data needs to be stored.

» Working with graphical images requires faster graphics cards to cope with the animation.

### Improving performance and cutting costs

In recent years, many manufacturers have invested in automated systems to speed up their processing. This has meant two things:

» goods can be produced faster

» it costs less to produce the goods – machines are cheaper to run and may be more reliable than people.

More employees can access the job market now that computers in the home enable them to work remotely.

FIGURE 1.60 **RAM sticks**

### DID YOU KNOW?

Random access memory (RAM) is a form of computer data storage, made up of circuits that allow the information stored (data) to be accessed in any order (randomly).

This is different to accessing data from storage devices such as tapes or discs that rely on a reading head. In these devices, the method of accessing the data takes longer.

Higher specification components make things happen faster (like the new style RAM shown in Figure 1.60).

There have been some unusual applications of technology. For example, some local councils have placed sensors into residents' rubbish bins to monitor what has been thrown away. The council then charges for collection and disposal of rubbish based on what is in residents' dustbins. In areas where this technology has been applied, there has been a rise in residents voluntarily recycling waste.

Sometimes, improving performance means adding functionality. For example, one of the most useful technical features on any website is the ability to search, which considerably reduces the time spent using the Internet. Implementing a search facility could improve the performance of the whole website and make it more usable.

### Responding to changing circumstances

There are times when organisations have no option but to respond to change, particularly if there is new legislation (new laws) with which the company must comply. In order to survive, companies need to respond to new opportunities, or changes in legislation. To do this, they must understand the market in which they operate, for example, by observing both what their competitors are doing and by monitoring their own product sales.

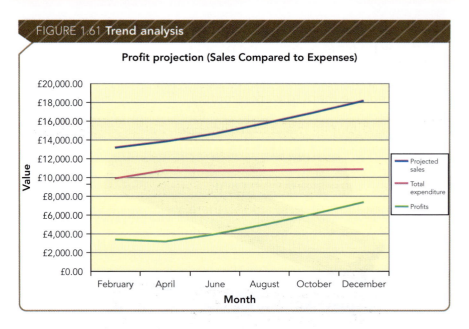

FIGURE 1.61 **Trend analysis**

**Profit projection (Sales Compared to Expenses)**

Trend analysis uses historic information about an organisation to help it understand how it has performed. This information helps managers identify where they might make savings or where there might be opportunities to improve sales.

Similarly, customer feedback can be collected and analysed and used, for example, to improve aspects of customer service. One method of improving service might be to create a website to provide:

» user information

» technical information

» health and safety information (if appropriate)

» additional information about other products

» FAQs (frequently asked questions)

» facility to contact the organisation.

In deciding which features to include on the website, the organisation will look at its activities and what it is trying to achieve through the website, and will choose functionality accordingly.

### Accessing new markets
As we have seen, being prepared to trade online will give organisations instant access to a large number of new markets:

» other parts of the UK

» other parts of Europe

» other parts of the world.

In addition, it allows the organisation to attract customers who might not go into shops because they are not able to, or because their shift pattern means shops are not open at the right times.

### Increasing sales/revenue

If organisations are able to improve their performance, reduce their costs and access new markets, there should be no reason why increased sales and improved profit figures should not follow.

### Improving internal/external communication

Before the development of modern technologies, organisations communicated internally using the telephone and memos.

FIGURE 1.62 **Sample memo**

---

**MEMO**

To:     Christen Baeur                     Date: 1st March 2008

From:  John Pitt

SUBJECT:   Monthly Meeting

---

Can you please ensure that you bring up-to-date sales figures for the Midlands to the monthly meeting on 6th March. If there are any problems, please let me know.

---

Memos were structured like emails but had to be delivered physically from one individual/department to another. In most organisations, this meant that deliveries were made once or twice a day. The advantage of email is that it is delivered electronically – it is sent and received instantly.

In addition, emails are now increasingly used for communicating with customers and suppliers, unless a formal letter is required. Mobile phones and Blackberry devices have made it possible for employees to stay in contact more easily with their office, customers and colleagues.

**TEAMWORK**

With a group of classmates, visit a website and discuss how you think you would improve it. Of all the suggestions that are made, select three improvements that you think should be a priority. Create a PowerPoint presentation that explains your choices to a virtual client.

**ASK**

The following are company websites where you can buy computer components, peripherals or whole systems.

http://www.ebuyer.com/

http://www.microdirect.co.uk/

http://www.planetmicro.co.uk/

Choose one website and make a list of what you think is a good example of one of each of the following:

* computer

* laptop

* printer

* scanner.

Write down the make and model information, or a brief description of the specification for each of the items, then find the same or similar products on the other two websites and compare the prices. Decide which company you would buy each item from.

List your choices and add the prices together to give a total required spending amount. Discuss these with your teacher/tutor.

# I want to be...

## ...a systems analyst

**Name:** Abi Zentu

**Age:** 34

**» What does a systems analyst do?**

I analyse an existing system and explain how it is used and suggest how it can be improved. It is useful if I have an understanding of the organisation as it helps me to tell the system designer about what is required.

Typically, I'll look at the organisation's current systems including their hardware, software and what they need to do with it. For example, a finance department will want to pay wages, or create or pay invoices.

To get reliable information, I talk to the people who use the systems and look at the sort of documents they work on. I then think about how the systems can be made more efficient. Sometimes I'll suggest upgrading hardware and/or software and changing the way things are processed.

**» What skills do you need?**

You have to be good at talking to people and working out what they really need, and what are just 'wish lists'! Then you have to think about what is going to be best for the organisation. I work as part of a team that includes a designer so I always have to think what information is going to help her create the new system. Because I work for myself and have to visit several clients, I need good time-management skills as well.

**» What qualifications have you got and did they help you get your job?**

Most systems analysts have higher qualifications. I did a BTEC HND, but mostly I learnt through the work I was doing with different companies. I've been in the business for about ten years now and decided to go freelance about a year ago. Before that I was working for a major banking organisation.

✱ Abi Zentu

# Case Study

BandStuff.com →

BandStuff.com is a small company employing 26 staff. They are based in Bradleyhead, where they are renting a commercial unit on an industrial estate.

The 26 staff have the following job roles:

» 2 managers

» 1 receptionist

» 2 accounts staff (one does the wages, the other keeps the accounts)

» 2 distribution staff

» 3 sales staff

» 4 packing staff

» 1 purchasing clerk

» 11 production staff.

There is a small network of seven linked computers in various places in the building, which the staff share. The production staff do not really need to use the computers, so the seven machines are generally used by the remaining 15 staff. At busy times, this has sometimes proved to be problematic.

The company produces band-related merchandise for some of the biggest artists in the UK. Merchandise includes items such as:

» t-shirts

» hoodies

» wristbands

» scarves.

They also sell accessories such as:

» calendars

» mugs

» pencil cases

» skateboards

» backpacks

» belts.

When the company first started, they only sold their products at gigs, and were limited to within a 100-mile radius of the company's Bradleyhead base. In 2005, BandStuff built a website that acted as a simple brochure for the company's merchandise. It contained a phone number and an email address and customers wishing to purchase goods would simply email or phone the company to place the order. Payment could be made to BandStuff.com only by cheque, which meant they were unable to accept credit card transactions.

The company is moderately successful, but they would like to grow.

## Questions

1) In your opinion, does the company have enough IT resources to respond to customers if their demand grows? Why?

2) Is the company making best use of its website? Why?

3) How could the company improve its IT resources?

4) How could the company improve its website?

# ✓ Assessment Tips

You will be assessed for this unit by taking an external examination.

You should prepare for this by making your own notes about the key areas of the unit and you should discuss these subjects with your teachers/tutors and other learners.

# SUMMARY / SKILLS CHECK

## » The basic components of technology systems

✓ Over the last 25 years, technology has developed rapidly and we now use computers and computer devices increasingly to do things we would previously have done manually, such as record keeping, trading and communicating.

✓ Understanding the basic components of systems and being able to identify the role of a variety of devices is essential for employees who want to work in jobs that use IT, or in jobs that support the use of IT.

✓ This unit has introduced you to the range of components, to input and output devices, methods of storing data and a range of communications options.

## » How the technology is used by organisations

✓ You have been introduced to different types of organisations and gained an understanding of how technology systems are used to support a variety of activities.

✓ You will now be able to link specific types of systems to organisations; for example, you should understand that some systems are more likely to be used by particular types of organisations, such as CAD/CAM systems being used in manufacturing, but not in banking, and ATMs being used in banking but not in transport and logistics.

✓ This will help you to make assumptions about organisations and what sorts of systems they are likely to use, based on what you know they do.

## » Why organisations implement and improve technology systems

✓ Because technology will continue to develop, and because the needs and activities of organisations change, a valuable IT employee understands a range of reasons why systems should be improved and how this can be achieved.

✓ These issues might be proactive (things the organisation is thinking about for the future, such as wanting to access new markets), or reactive (things the organisation must respond to in order to operate, such as changes in legislation).

✓ As an employee, you might find yourself being asked to think about how the organisation can be improved through the use of IT on a larger scale, across the organisation, for example, or maybe on a smaller scale, if you are asked whether there is an aspect of your own role that could be improved through the implementation of IT.

# OVERVIEW

How is technology changing the way that people work and spend their leisure time? How does it affect the way organisations work? Why do organisations and individuals choose one type of technology over another? And how does technology affect society? In this unit you'll discover the answer to all of these questions.

It used to be that only large, rich companies could afford the latest technology. But over time, as the latest technology has become cheaper, smaller companies have also been able to use it. Bar codes and electronic scanning used to be something you only saw in large supermarkets, but now it's in most corner shops. And the corner shop is also likely to have the latest security technology, such as closed-circuit television and smoke/fire alarms.

Photocopiers, fax machines, wireless hotspots, the Internet, etc. have all helped transform working life. Barcode scanners, online shopping, etc. have all helped transform shopping. Simulations, interactive learning, online teaching and testing, etc. have helped transform learning. And broadband Internet, cable television, gadgets such as the iPod, mobile phones, etc. have all helped transform leisure life.

Technology also means that much of the above – working, shopping, learning, leisure – can now be done without even having to leave your own home.

But at the same time that many people are able to make full use of technological developments, many others are being left behind, either because they can't afford the latest technology or because they live and/or work in an area that can't receive it.

# 02

# The Impact of Technology

## Skills list

By the end of this unit, you should:

» know how and why organisations use technology

» know about the impact of technology on individuals and society

## Job watch

There are many jobs that make use of these skills, including:

» systems analyst

» product designer

# Know how and why organisations use technology

**O**rganisations can be classified in three main types:

» Public sector

» Private sector

» Voluntary sector.

## What does each of these classifications mean?

### Public sector

Public sector organisations are owned by the public. This means that they are generally financed through the taxes people pay to the government. Even though the public own these organisations, they have no direct influence on how they operate. The government ultimately controls these organisations through a range of agencies. Any profit made through the operation of these organisations is reinvested into the organisation.

Public sector organisations include the national government and local government (sometimes referred to as councils).

FIGURE 2.1 Leisure centre booking through a website

In some towns and cities in the UK, leisure centres are owned and controlled by local councils. Figure 2.1 shows Purbeck Council's website page for users to book sports centre facilities.

### Private sector

These are organisations owned by individuals, or groups of individuals. The purpose of private sector organisations is to make a profit for their owners. Sometimes the profits are shared by the owners, and sometimes the profits are reinvested to help the organisation to grow and thereby make more profit.

### Voluntary sector

Voluntary sector organisations also aim to make profits – with the intention of using any profits made to help others.

**TEAMWORK**

**With a group of classmates, create a short PowerPoint presentation that explains the difference between public sector, private sector and voluntary sector organisations, giving three examples of each type of organisation.**

As a group, present this to your teacher/tutor or to the remainder of your class.

## How organisations use technology

It is hard to imagine how organisations existed before the introduction of technology. Many tasks, such as writing letters and compiling lists of data, had to be done manually.

All important papers were kept as hard copy and stored in large filing cabinets that occupied much of the floor space in offices. Medical records were written by hand and stored in large brown envelopes in a filing cabinet. Medical records were often lost when people moved from one area to another as all the brown envelopes containing their records had to be sent by post to their new doctor.

The following are examples of areas where technology has improved efficiency.

### Administration

The range of technology that now exists to support administration is vast and, to cover it fully, would need a book in its own right.

In your work placement, find at least four examples of technology that are used and ask to be shown how to use each one.

Write up your experiences into a short leaflet under the heading **Technology in Administration**.

FIGURE 2.2
Photocopier

The following are some examples, but remember the list is not exhaustive – there are many more!

» **Photocopiers:** The main use of photocopiers is to make duplicate documents. Copiers that print in colour can also duplicate photographs or other colour images.

Some photocopiers can be linked to a computer network and can act as a printer. Digital files are sent directly from the PC to the photocopier for printing.

» **Scanners:** There are various types of scanner, the most commonly used is a flatbed scanner. Scanners work in much the same way as a photocopier – the scanner makes a digital image of the document which can be stored electronically. This image can be attached to an email and sent to someone else, or it can simply be stored.

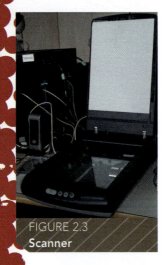

FIGURE 2.3
Scanner

» **Fax machines:** These are regularly used in business to send documents over a telephone line. The image that is transmitted is a copy of the original that is digitised, sent and reassembled through the receiving fax machine.

This is a very useful way to send documents that have been annotated by hand or which carry signatures, although the invention of scanners means that this can also be done by attaching a scanned document to an email.

» **Printers:** There are a variety of printers currently on the market, including inkjet and laser printers. Inkjet printers are those that create an image by spraying tiny drops of ink onto the page to make the image. Laser printers use a laser beam and toner (a dry type of ink) to burn an image onto the paper.

FIGURE 2.4
Fax machine

» **Telephone systems:** Telephone systems can now be linked to networks and may have additional functions from those you would normally expect from a telephone system. For example, the Cisco system shown in Figure 2.6 not only takes messages but, through its network links, emails the recipient to alert them that a voice message is stored. It then allows the user to listen to the message through the phone itself, or via the computer.

FIGURE 2.5
Printer

» **Databases:** These are used to store large quantities of information in a structured way electronically so that the data can be searched, sorted and manipulated in a variety of ways that an organisation would find useful.

Let's imagine that you have a database of customer records for a book club. Each record contains the following information:

» forename

» last name

» street

» town

» county

» postcode

» telephone number

» date of birth

» favourite subject.

FIGURE 2.6
Cisco phone

Let's think of five ways in which we might organise or use this data.

1. An alphabetical list of all customers arranged from A to Z, using the initial letter of their last name.

2. A list of all members who live in a particular town to send them information about a book fair.

3. A list of all members with a date of birth between two values to send them information about books for a specific age range.

4. A list of individuals who like a particular type of book so that the company can send them information about books for a chosen subject.

5. A full list of information excluding telephone number, date of birth and subject information to be used as a mailing list for a new book catalogue.

THINK

If you were going to create a database of all your family's DVDs or CDs, what information about the DVD or CD would you store?

Database systems are very important to organisations and Unit 5 of this book investigates the subject in full. The unit also gives you the opportunity to gain skills in developing database systems.

## Control and monitoring

FIGURE 2.7
Smoke alarm

» **Smoke/fire alarms:** These work very simply. They contain electronic sensors that detect smoke or heat. In the home, these alarms can be powered either from the electrical mains or by battery.

Once the sensor is activated, it triggers a piercing siren. The alarms are designed to alert anyone who is in the property to smoke or fire.

In large offices and factories, detectors will be placed throughout the building. They will be linked to a main board and monitored by a central point that will put in a call to the fire brigade if required.

» **Process control:** We considered process control from a manufacturing perspective in Unit 1, through the concept of robotic car manufacturing. Another example is an automated system that can be used commercially in market gardening.

It may not surprise you to learn that some plants, fruits and vegetables are grown under cover because the climate in the United Kingdom does not support them naturally.

In order to mimic the temperature and humidity in the countries where they usually grow, the greenhouses are monitored by computer systems using sensors. The systems spray water, turn

FIGURE 2.8 **Automated greenhouse**

heaters on or off, cover or uncover parts of the greenhouse, or open and close vents to simulate the plants' natural environment.

## Education and training

» **Simulations:** One of the best known uses of simulation is in aircraft pilot training. The pilot sits in a simulator that replicates the controls of an aircraft and a display monitor provides a visual representation of a particular flight path or airport.

The pilot can be given a series of tests and his or her reactions are monitored. If he or she fails, the test can be repeated.

FIGURE 2.9 **Flight simulation**

The main advantage of using a simulator in training is that the trainee never leaves the ground and any misjudgements are not fatal.

**» On-screen testing:** There has been an increase in use of computers to test skills in the classroom.

As shown in Figure 2.10, these tests are often multiple-choice, although they can also require the user to input an answer using the keypad.

**TRY THIS**

If you have never tried an on-screen test before, log onto the following website and try a Level 1 Literacy (English) or Numeracy (Maths) test.

www1.edexcel.org.uk/tot/alns2/CMA-Edexcel-web2.2.swf

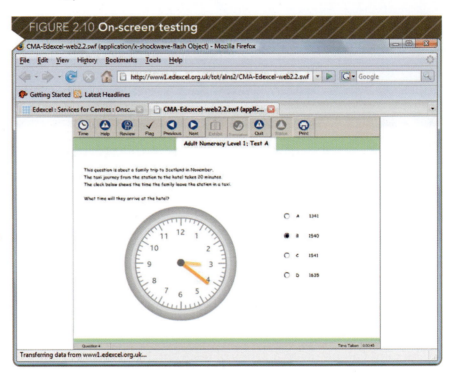

FIGURE 2.10 On-screen testing

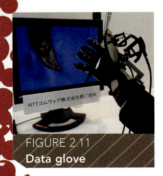

FIGURE 2.11
Data glove

**FIND OUT**

The technology for virtual reality systems is quite complex but is also very interesting. If you would like to know more, you might find the following website useful:

www.howstuffworks.com/

**» Virtual reality:** These systems simulate (imitate the appearance of) the real world. Using devices such as headsets, data gloves and body sensors, the computer tracks electronic points placed on the body and interprets the movements. This allows the player to appear to be inside a game.

**» VLEs:** VLE stands for Virtual Learning Environment. Computers can be used to create a way of learning in the form of a virtual classroom. It is e-learning.

In order to create a VLE, many schools and colleges download free VLE software. Moodle is the platform most often used (see Figure 2.12).

Teachers/tutors can place all kinds of learning activities including task sheets, exercises, multiple-choice tests, assignments and other useful information on the school or college site so that learners can access the content from inside the organisation, and from the comfort of their own homes.

FIGURE 2.12 **A moodle VLE**

## Mobile working

Technology has dramatically changed the way that we work – both by keeping us in constant contact with the office, customers or suppliers, and also in allowing us to work from almost anywhere.

» **Mobile phones:** Although different types of mobile phone have different uses, they all have one thing in common – the ability to make and receive telephone calls. Some have additional functions such as a camera or video recorder, voice recorder or MP3 player, and some even have the ability to access the Internet.

FIGURE 2.13
**Mobile phone**

» **PDAs:** A more sophisticated version of the personal digital assistant (PDA) is the Blackberry.

The primary use of the Blackberry is to send and receive emails, although it also supports text messaging, Internet browsing and some can be used as mobile phones.

Much like mobile phones, these devices function wherever they can receive a wireless signal.

## Wireless hotspots

A wireless hotspot is often a business location where customers are given free access to the Internet via wireless technology. The website shown in Figure 2.15 provides a directory of wireless hotspots in the UK, organised alphabetically by town.

FIGURE 2.14
**Blackberry**

FIGURE 2.15 **Directory of wireless hotspots in the UK**

» **GPS:** When used in transport and distribution, GPS systems are excellent at tracking parcels that are being moved from one location to another. Some systems are so accurate that a parcel's time of arrival can be predicted.

Travelling sales staff used to have to rely on maps to get to places they had nor previously visited. They would either have to learn the route before leaving home or they'd have to keep stopping to check the map. Now they can use a GPS device such as TomTom to find the organisation they want to visit. The GPS system gives instructions about where, and when, to turn right or left, which exit to take on a traffic island and so on.

» **Bleepers:** The first bleeper systems did little more than bleep. The user then had to find a phone to contact a call centre to pick up their message. Newer bleepers have small display screens so that users can read the message without having to find a phone.

### Marketing

» **Websites:** Each time a user accesses a website, it is known as a hit. A website can be set up so that each hit on that site can be recorded. The system can also record which pages of the website were accessed or which products were viewed. Organisations can use this information to add pop-ups to the most popular pages so that when these are accessed advertisements will literally pop up on the screen.

Blocking pop-ups is easy. If you are using Internet Explorer, you can choose to turn the pop-up blocker on and off through the Tools menu.

Similarly, if you are using Mozilla you can tick the option to block the pop-up windows (see Figure 2.18).

FIGURE 2.16
**Bleeper or Pager**

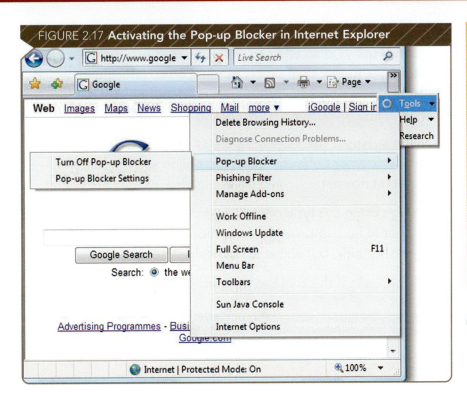

FIGURE 2.17 **Activating the Pop-up Blocker in Internet Explorer**

A web browser is a piece of software that allows a user to display and interact with information such as text, images, videos and music on a website. The appearance of a web page may differ between browsers.

Web browsers include Mozilla Firefox, Safari, Konqueror, Opera, Flock, Internet Explorer, Epiphany and AOL Explorer

FIGURE 2.18 **Activating the pop-up Blocker in Mozilla**

With both browsers you still have the option to create exceptions. This means that you can decide to allow pop-ups for some websites but block the rest.

» **Touch-screen displays:** Some marketing activities use touch-screen displays in an effort to make the user experience more interactive. Rather than simply reading an advertisement which is largely a passive activity, the user is encouraged to explore the advert using touch-screen technology.

» **Online surveys:** The increasing use of online surveys has seen the development of websites where online surveys can be created at no cost.

Through using this type of service, it suggests that organisations will benefit from improved information, not only about what customers think, but about what their employees think.

This means that this tool can be used in a variety of ways.

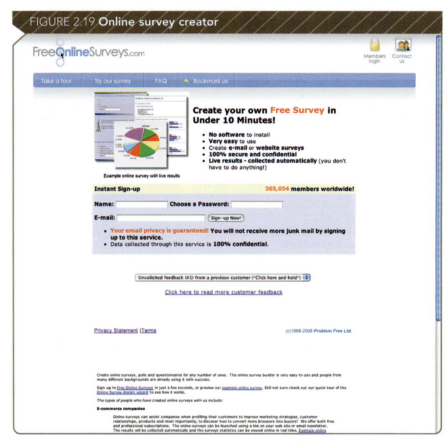

FIGURE 2.19 **Online survey creator**

» **Desktop publishing (DTP):** Software such as Microsoft Publisher now has a range of templates that can be used to create different types of publication. In the example shown in Figure 2.20 you will notice that, in addition to the advertisement templates shown, there are templates for calendars, flyers, business cards and even envelopes.

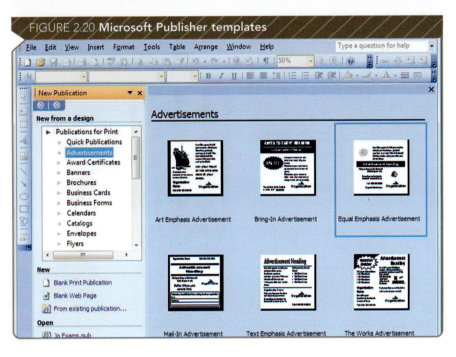

FIGURE 2.20 Microsoft Publisher templates

**DID YOU KNOW?**

A template is a guide or model for a document. It usually includes default settings for format (such as font and colour) and positioning of components in the document (such as headings and images).

This does not mean that these details cannot be changed by the user – it just means the user has a starting point for the type of document chosen or required.

## Sales

» **EPOS:** EPOS (Electronic Point of Sale) systems are used in shops to record sales transactions. The bar code of each item sold is scanned. This removes the item from stock records and adds the cost of the item to the customer's bill.

In the same way, if an item is returned, it is scanned back into stock and the customer receives a refund.

» **Credit card readers:** If the customer pays for goods or services using a card, the payment information is recorded through a credit card reader. The customer inserts their card and PIN (Personal Identification Number). If the PIN is correct, the system will ensure that the bank or credit card company authorises the payment and the transaction is complete.

» **Smart displays:** A smart display is a touch-activated and controlled screen that acts as a computer monitor. As it uses wireless technology, it can be carried around a building completely separate from the base unit and used to surf the net or play games. In fact, it works best for any use that does not require keyboard input, although a touch-controlled keyboard can be activated on the screen if needed.

» **Online shopping:** Many organisations offer customers the opportunity to buy online, including most of the larger supermarkets. Clothes and shoe shops also offer online facilities.

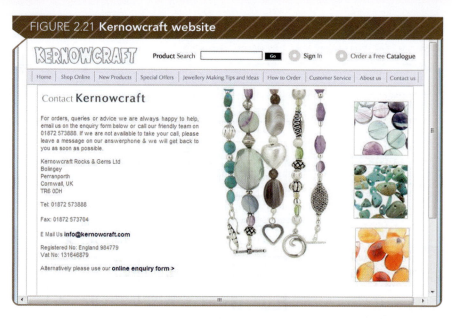

FIGURE 2.21 **Kernowcraft website**

But one of the most important developments achieved through online shopping is that it is easier to access unusual items. The website shown in Figure 2.21 is for Kernowcraft, a small business that sells gemstones and settings for jewellery making. In this particular situation, Kernowcraft benefits from being able to access a much larger customer base, and customers benefit from being able to buy these items more readily and at any time of the day or night.

» **Loyalty cards:** Some shops issue loyalty cards to encourage customers to keep buying from a particular store. Each purchase gives the customer a number of points that are added to a running total. These points can then be exchanged for a range of vouchers or gifts.

FIGURE 2.22
**Loyalty cards**

**ASK**

Talk to family members and find out how many different types of loyalty cards they have.

Make a list and place the list in your portfolio.

**LINKS**

## Security

» **CCTV:** Closed Circuit Television (CCTV) systems are used in many different ways by a variety of organisations. For example, most town centres have CCTV systems that monitor the activity of individuals and groups.

Many schools and colleges have CCTV in their buildings or grounds to monitor people entering and leaving the premises.

Some travel companies use CCTV inside trains, buses and aircraft to provide security for travellers. Similarly, smaller shops with only one or two employees often have CCTV as a deterrent against theft or anti-social behaviour.

In many situations, the CCTV images are recorded and/or monitored by security teams. If criminal or dangerous activity takes place, these teams either deal directly with the problem or, if the situation is more serious, call in the police. The CCTV footage can be stored and used in any legal proceedings.

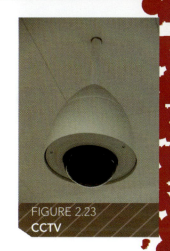

FIGURE 2.23
CCTV

**TEAMWORK**

Together with two or three classmates, create a leaflet about technology used for security. Create your leaflet using a DTP (desktop publishing) software package such as Microsoft Publisher.

Print your leaflet and put it in your portfolio.

Re-open the original file you created for your leaflet, and make five changes to the document (this could be font size or type, colour or position of images). Print a second copy and add to your portfolio

**LINKS**

» **Anti-theft tags:** These come in a variety of forms, but they serve a very simple function. In the event that someone attempts to steal an item, a sensor on it is activated and an alarm sounds alerting staff to the situation.

For example, anti-theft tags in library books are carefully inserted into the book's cover – often in the form of a magnetic strip in the book's spine. Library staff are alerted when someone attempts to take the book out of the library without the strip being deactivated.

» **Access cards:** Access to rooms or areas of a building has traditionally been controlled by keys. This is not a good method of controlling movement as keys can be lost, or individuals with access keys leave the organisation and forget to return the key. This means that organisations can never be sure of total security because there is no way to be absolutely sure how many keys exist that will still operate the locks.

BANDSTUFF.com

FIGURE 2.24
Room access card

FIGURE 2.25
Room clicker

FIGURE 2.26
Movement sensor

The invention of swipe cards revolutionised access control. The data held on the card's stripe can be modified to include access codes for areas of a building that the cardholder is allowed to enter. If someone leaves and takes their card with them, the organisation simply changes the access codes to the rooms or areas affected. It is less important for the employee to return their card.

This system is often used in hotels as an alternative to room keys.

Another device used is the access button. It is programmed in the same way as an access card and is passed over the lock, or pressed, to open the door.

» **Movement detectors:** These contain electronic sensors that detect body heat or movement (depending on the type). If the alarm is set and the sensor detects body heat or movement, the alarm will be triggered.

## Reasons for using technology

There are many reasons why organisations introduce technology, such as, to:

» improve communication

» improve efficiency

» access new markets

» increase profits.

### Improving communication
Fast and efficient communications are the lifeblood of organisations, whether they are large businesses or a small group of individuals working together on a project. Technology has made it easier for staff to communicate with each other both inside and outside the office setting. Improving communications with suppliers and customers improves overall efficiency.

### Improving efficiency
One of the main benefits of using technology is to improve efficiency. This may be achieved in a number of ways:

» speed increased – jobs can be done faster than they could manually

» throughput increased – because jobs can be done faster, more jobs can be done in the same amount of time

» fewer staff needed – when processes are automated, fewer staff may be needed to complete the tasks.

### Accessing new markets

The development of sales opportunities through the application of technologies,  such as the Internet, has allowed businesses to access new markets anywhere in the world that uses the same technology.

A business with a website can be active 24 hours a day, 7 days a week, 52 weeks of the year and customers will be able to buy products from around the world.

FIGURE 2.27 **The global market**

### Increasing profits

Improvement in efficiency almost always means lower costs and increased profits. If processing speed and throughput are increased, more orders can be filled and more goods packed for distribution. The immediate effect is that goods will get to customers faster and therefore payments should be received more quickly.

A hidden benefit of improved efficiency is that, if goods and services get to customers more quickly, then more business may come from those customers. Also, additional business may come from their friends, family and other businesses that they have told about the excellent service – potentially further increasing profits.

## Individuals

Technology has had an effect on many different aspects of our lives. It has had an impact on the way we live, how we learn, how we are employed and the way in which we work, and the ways in which we socialise.

Let's consider some of these affects.

### *Living*

» **Entertainment and leisure:** One of the most compelling ways in which technology has affected our lives is in the way we are entertained or we choose to entertain ourselves.

Computer technology exists all around us in the devices we use every day.

Examples of devices people use everyday include:
- mobile phones
- MP3 players or iPods
- Hand-held computer devices such as PDAs (Personal Digital Assistants)
- games machines such as the Xbox 360, the Sony PSP or PlayStation.

FIGURE 2.28
Xbox 360

JOIN IN

**Talk to your friends or classmates. How many examples of technology can you identify that you use for entertainment?**

At school or college you will use computer networks, the Internet, computer software such as spreadsheet packages, PC games, desktop publishing software and peripherals (equipment attached to computers) such as printers, graphics tablets, plotters and scanners.

It is important to understand that you will also be using many of these to pursue your leisure interests. Graphics tablets can be used, for example, to make digital pictures. The Internet can be surfed to gather information about hobbies and interests. You will use messaging software to communicate with your friends.

**THINK**

Identify some of the technologies you use regularly for entertainment or leisure. Draw a table that has a column for each of the following three headings:

Technology

Description

What you use it for

Fill in your table: name the technology, give a short description of it and write a brief explanation of what you use it for.

**LINKS**

Create a short PowerPoint presentation entitled 'Using technology for fun' and present it to your teacher.

Print a copy and put it in your portfolio.

» **E-safety:** It is essential that you use the Internet sensibly. Accessing certain parts of the Internet can be dangerous. Your school or college will have made some decisions and implemented systems designed to prevent you from accessing unsuitable materials or websites. Your parents or guardians may also have applied some parental locks to parts of your system.

**TEAMWORK**

With a group of friends or classmates, research the following websites and create an A5 booklet that gives guidance to 11 to 16 year olds on the safe use of the Internet.

www.ceop.gov.uk/

www.thinkuknow.co.uk/

www.bbc.co.uk/cbbc/help/safesurfing/

www.childnet-int.org/

www.chatdanger.com/

**LINKS**

Use the information from your research for the teamwork task to create an A3 poster that gives at least five 'Golden Rules' about the safe use of the Internet. Put it on your classroom wall.

FIGURE 2.29 **Website safety symbols**

**» Privacy:** Technology has had two major impacts on privacy. We are more likely to put personal information into systems if we do so from the comfort of our own homes. As such, it is essential that we remember that, once entered into the system, this information may well be accessible to others; some of whom might use the information for inappropriate activities. For this reason, we should never provide any information unless we know that a website is safe. If you are unsure about the safety of a website, the symbols shown in Figure 2.29 will give you an indication of how secure it is.

The padlock shown in the closed position indicates that a website is secure for you to input your personal details. The padlock in the unlocked position indicates that information can be seen by third parties.

Care should be taken about how much information you input on social networking websites. In particular, you should not include information about your age, location or gender. Use a nickname rather than your own name and make sure that you only talk to people you know. Talking to strangers can be dangerous.

**» Travel:** Many people think that the Internet has made the world much smaller. Users have the ability to find out more about other places around the world, whereas before they had to rely on library books and travel brochures to see images of exotic places. Now you can see pictures of faraway places, and real-time images of some places. For example, pictures of New York Times Square can be viewed through Earthcam (see www.earthcam.com/usa/newyork/timessquare/).

**» Communication:** In Unit 1 we considered different ways that technology can be used to communicate such as mobile phones, email and messaging services. But what about VOIP (Voice Over Internet Protocol) services such as Skype?

Skype is a little bit different. Users can talk over the Internet using a microphone and headset. They can call someone who has a Skype account and communicate for free. In reality, they are paying for the call because they are paying for their Internet connection. However, as they would have the connection anyway, it is fair to say that the service is effectively free.

Through the service, you can call mobile or landline numbers and send SMS messages but you have to first buy credits.

FIGURE 2.30 **Skype**

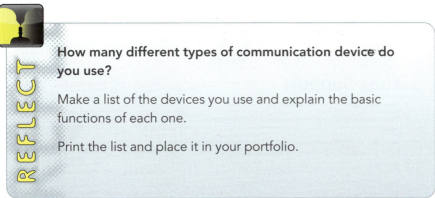

**REFLECT**

**How many different types of communication device do you use?**

Make a list of the devices you use and explain the basic functions of each one.

Print the list and place it in your portfolio.

## Learning

Through the use of technology, we have access to many more ways of learning. We can learn through the Internet, through VLEs (as explained earlier in this unit), through simulation and virtual reality.

This has meant that we are no longer limited to studying in the home or classroom; we can learn anywhere where computers exist. We have greater access to information because, in addition to being able to look up factual information, we can also find different views on that information.

Let's take the example of buying a laptop computer.

If you access websites such as www.pcworld.co.uk you can find a number of different laptop models in a particular price range. Clicking on the link entitled 'View full product information' will take you to another page where you can read the technical specification for the product. In this instance, it provides you with a list of the components in the laptop and explains the benefits of some of them. You can then search for the laptop on the Internet and read comparisons with other similar models, or you can look up a particular component and find out what other users think about it.

To  learn how to use a product you might search the Internet for user manuals or web pages that offer advice and guidance, like the one shown in Figure 2.31 for Xbox systems. In this instance, in addition to system and accessory information, there is information about the games that can be purchased for this platform.

FIGURE 2.31 **Xbox registration website**

Learning is not always about acquiring knowledge as part of a course of study; many people like to learn for pleasure. However, the development of technology has, in part, offered additional ways to access learning and gain qualifications.

The on-screen multiple choice test you were asked to experiment with earlier in this unit is a mock test for a real qualification.

LearnDirect™ is an organisation specialising in qualifications that can be gained solely online. The types of courses that can be studied include languages, business management and IT. For further information see the following URL: www.learndirect.co.uk/

The advantage of learning through the use of technology is that you can effectively learn at any time, in any place, anywhere in the world that has access to that technology.

## Work

» **Types of job:** Most jobs will probably require some sort of basic IT skills. A nurse needs access to computerised medical records. A music teacher who travels from school to school may well use an electronic diary on a PDA to keep track of when and where they need to be for lessons. A builder or electrician might use an accounting package to prepare invoices and keep accounts. There is no getting away from it – computers are everywhere!

The range of jobs in the information technology industry is wide and varied. Table 2.1 shows some examples of how these can be organised into some general categories, which can be further broken down into a range of particular roles.

**FIND OUT**

Choose one of the job types listed in Table 2.1 that is of particular interest to you. Carry out some Internet research and find an advertisement for your chosen job.

Print the advertisement and put it in your portfolio. Discuss the job with your tutor or teacher.

**TABLE 2.1 Job roles in the IT industry**

| Category | Type of job | Description |
|---|---|---|
| Installer/Engineer | System builder<br><br>Network installer<br><br>Network engineer | With these jobs, employees are working with hardware. They will be building computer base units, installing cabling, connecting devices. In some cases they will also install software. |
| Analyst | Systems analyst<br><br>Business analyst | Employees in these roles will be working with existing systems. They will look at what the organisation does and establish whether their existing system solution is appropriate for their needs and if not, they will design solutions. |
| Technician | Help desk support or<br><br>desktop analyst | Technicians do not usually get involved in installation activities – they will help users. They will repair simple faults and carry out system upgrades once a system has been installed. |
| Administrator | Database administrator/ manager | A database administrator will be responsible for ensuring that the structure of a database works correctly. They will often design the reports that extract information from the database. They will probably also be responsible for setting up the user permissions that allow different employees to access different screens or types of records. |
| Developer | Product designer | These employees will be developing new products. They will design new devices or computer components. They will develop new functionality or ways of using components or devices. |
| Programmer | System/application programmers | Most programmers will be able to work on both systems programs and applications programs, depending on the task in hand. Systems programs are those who get the components to work together. They will write programs that control the computer system's resources. They might even write operating systems. Applications programmers create programs for users, such as a word processing program, chat software or a spreadsheet. |

**» Ways of working:** We have considered how technology is used in an office or organisational setting. There are other ways of working that have been made possible through the development of technology. For example, employers are increasingly allowing their employees to work from home. They do this for a number of reasons:

1. It gives the employer a wider range of potential employees to choose from (for example, carers, the disabled).

2. Employers do not need so much office space, so apart from spending money initially to get the home worker set up and running, there is no further outlay for premises.

3. Many employers feel that employees are more productive when they work from home because they can work at times that suit them.

4. Some people argue that these employees will also be less stressed because they do not have to travel to and from work.

The technology that allows individuals to work from home is straightforward. They require a computer or a laptop, a broadband modem (to link to the Internet) and access to the organisation's systems, possibly through a web interface. The employee needs other essential items such as a printer or scanner, a desk and a chair. Most employers also provide a telephone – either a landline or a mobile phone or, in some cases, both.

Having employees work from home has vastly increased the number of employees available, and has also enabled individuals unable to leave the home to contribute to the world of work in a positive way.

**» Skills set:** The skills needed to work with technology will depend on which technologies are used and how they are used. However, the following is a simple list of desirable skills for anyone using computerised systems.

Hardware tasks:

– switching on and off

– how to use the basic technology

– how to use any peripheral devices that link to the main device

– how to run CDs or DVDs

– how to carry out basic maintenance on equipment (such as replace ink cartridges in printers).

Software tasks:

– opening and closing programs

– how to save work

– how to use menus

– how to run individual software applications

– how to integrate different applications

– how to send and receive email.

Internet tasks:

– how to collect information from a variety of sources, including the Internet

– how to access the Internet and carry out basic searches.

General tasks:

– how to organise files and folders

– how to access self-help support materials

– how to respond to simple error messages

– simple fault finding techniques

**REFLECT**

**Think about the lists of skills that have been identified here.**

How many of these skills do you think you already have? Make a record of your IT skills using the list shown as a basic checklist.

When you think about those you do not have, which do you think are important?

Talk to your teacher or tutor about this.

@work

Before your work experience, find out what you will be doing and see if you can identify two new skills you will be able to learn.

### Socialising

**» Virtual communities:** A virtual community is a group of individuals in contact with each other over a period of time, usually by email, letter, phone or maybe through chatrooms. These individuals will usually share a common concern or interest. This might be as diverse as: baseball cards, motorcycles, computer programming, guitars, a particular band or singer, gardening, sailing or stamp collecting.

It is possible that the individuals involved in the community will never meet, although there are exceptions. These communities continue as long as there are members interested in keeping the group active.

**» Social networking:** Social networking sites are similar to virtual communities, but are likely to be targeted at particular age groups rather than specific interests.

The most popular social networking sites are currently:

– Bebo  www.Bebo.com

– MSN Livespaces http://home.services.spaces.live.com/

– Facebook  www.facebook.com/

– MySpace  www.myspace.com/

People using these sites often do so to socialise. They will often talk to friends they already know, but can also make new friends.

### DID YOU KNOW?

Take great care about communicating with people you don't already know personally.

People might try to mislead you and claim to be something or someone that they are not. Think very carefully before agreeing to meet someone you have met on the Internet. Always seek advice from your parents or guardians or a trustworthy adult if someone suggests you meet them.

# Society

The impact of technology on society in general can be considered from a number of different perspectives. For the purposes of this course, we will consider three direct ways in which technology has had an impact:

» globalisation

» digital divide

» e-citizenship.

### Globalisation

Technology has enabled far more interaction between different countries and nationalities. Many people claim that the world is getting smaller and in some ways it probably is. For example, the cost of communicating with people in other parts of the world has become cheaper, and it has become possible to trade across national borders and cultural boundaries.

### Digital divide

In the UK there are individuals who possess IT skills and are able to use technology systems with relative ease. There are also those who have no IT skills and who have little or no access to technology and who might be overwhelmed by it, or disadvantaged by lack of it.

This has created a society of people who are divided by either their possession of or lack of IT skills, and their ability to use modern IT systems. On a larger scale, this can affect entire countries or communities where technology is still too expensive and is beyond the means of many individuals.

In the UK there are people who have never used IT and who might feel left out by a generation who have been using IT since they were in primary school.

### E-citizenship

People that have access to technology and have the right skills to use it can be said to have e-citizenship – they are citizens of the e-world. If you are not already a member, by the end of your Diploma you, too, will be a citizen of the e-world!

# ...a product designer

**Name:** Toni Dziadulewicz

**Age:** 42

## » What does a product designer do?

We develop technological products. These might be completely new products, which we design from scratch and then see through to production, or they might be something that finds a new way of using an existing product. Or we might be given an existing product and asked to add new functionality or compact it down into a new, smaller unit with extra features.

## » What prompts your ideas?

Sometimes it's just from being creative and sitting down and thinking about a product and how it could be improved, or reading about a new technological development and wondering how it could be applied to different situations or existing products. But sometimes we're approached by a company or an individual to find a solution to a specific problem or to develop an idea.

## » What skills does a product designer need?

The main thing is to be creative and able to come up with lots of good design ideas. But you also need good communication skills and teamwork skills, so that you can share your ideas with other people and receive feedback and suggestions. It helps to be able to make sketches or write descriptions of new products and to be able to make prototypes or models of them. It also helps to have a good understanding of technology!

## » What qualifications do product designers need?

Most of us have been through higher education, which means we have a degree, a Foundation Degree or a BTEC Higher National. But it's also important to gain experience and build up a portfolio of work or, at the very least, ideas. If you're creative and work hard, it's possible to get a good job without going through higher education.

✳ Toni Dziadulewicz

# Case Study

## BandStuff.com

The managers at BandStuff.com have been looking at their IT systems and have decided to advertise for two new staff – one to work as a database administrator and the other as a helpdesk support analyst to provide support to all the company's IT users. Both of these will be junior roles.

Before advertising these posts, the managers have asked you to investigate each of these roles and write a short description of what each post requires the employee to do. Give an indication of the salary you would expect the successful candidate to earn (remember that this is a junior post).

You may well find the following websites useful:

www.fish4.co.uk/iad/jobs

www.jobserve.com/

www.theitjobboard.com/

The jobs will be similar, regardless of where in the UK the individuals are employed. However, there is likely to be a variation in salary depending on location.

To make this a more relevant exercise you should assume that BandStuff.com is based in your own home town or county.

Write up your findings as a two-slide presentation with notes and share with your tutor or teacher.

# ✓Assessment Tips

For this unit you will need to present a portfolio which will be a combination of coursework assignments, classwork and activities. Your teacher/tutor will award marks for the work you have submitted across three mark bands.

## Task One: Technology in organisations

You will be given an assignment that asks you to find out about the technology that is used by two different and contrasting organisations. You will be asked to describe the range of technologies that they use and explain how and why they use them. It is recommended that you use examples of real organisations rather than fictitious ones.

## Task Two: The impact of technology on individuals and society

In a second assignment you will be asked to give examples of the ways in which technology affects how we live, learn, work and socialise as individuals. Again you will need to give real examples and give brief explanations in each category.

You will then expand your assignment to consider how technology impacts on society as a whole, giving examples of some of the issues that affect us all.

# SUMMARY / SKILLS CHECK

**» Why and how do organisations use technology?**

✓ Expanding on what you have learned in Unit 1, you will have further developed your understanding of the uses of technology by considering some of its functional uses in more depth. You will have been introduced to a wider range of technologies and you should now be able to talk confidently about a range of devices and systems.

**» The impact of technology on individuals and society**

✓ This section is particularly important, as you will have reflected on the benefits and possibly on some drawbacks of the development of technology. You will be able to show that you understand how technology affects our lives, the way we work, learn and socialise, and you will be able to show that you understand the effect of this both on the individual and on society as a whole.

# OVERVIEW

Whatever profession learners work in, there will always be an aspect of their work where they will need to communicate clearly with people, either face-to-face or by email, telephone or facsimile.

This unit discusses in detail why communication is so important in the IT industry and business in general. It looks at the different methods people use to communicate and how to choose the best method for a particular purpose. Learners will look at how using IT can help get the message across if you communicate clearly and listen to one another.

Many learners will have belonged to a sporting team at one point in their lives and will therefore understand the importance of teamwork, supporting each other to produce positive results.

This unit will help learners to discover the different types of people within a team and how a person's behaviour and actions, positive or negative, can affect the whole team's performance.

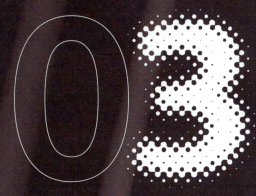

# Working with People

## Skills list

**By the end of this unit, you should:**

» Know how and why different types of communication media are used for different business purposes

» Be able to use clear appropriate English and demonstrate numeracy skills in a range of simple business related communications

» Know how behaviour, personal styles and actions affect communication and achievement of objectives

» Be able to work in a team to meet agreed objectives, demonstrating active listening skills and effective, confident speaking skills

» Be able to reflect on the workings of teams and the different roles individuals play within teams, demonstrating self awareness.

## Job watch

**Examples of jobs that involve working with people include:**

» administrator
» help desk assistant
» systems analyst
» product designer
» database developer
» database administrator
» website designer
» computer games designer
» multimedia editor.

# Know how and why different types of communication media are used for different business purposes

Communication media is the title that is used to describe all types of devices and methods of sending and receiving information.

There are three types or categories of communication media and each category has a number of technologies (different methods of communication).

## Electronic media

Electronic media include the following:

» websites

» blogs

» emails

» text messaging.

### Websites
Websites communicate visually (with pictures and graphics), in writing (through text) and through sound (as some websites have links to videos or other movie files).

### Blogs
The term blog is an abbreviation of the term weblog. These websites are usually made up of newsletters or diary entries by individuals that are updated on a regular basis. Usually, the owner of the website has to invite others to view the content, although this is not always the case.

### Emails
Emails are one of the commonest forms of communication. To send and receive emails you need an email account.

Whilst you can certainly abbreviate the text in emails when you are sending them to friends, when it comes to business-related emails they must be clear and easy to understand and you must take care to proofread them before sending to ensure that the spelling and grammar is correct.

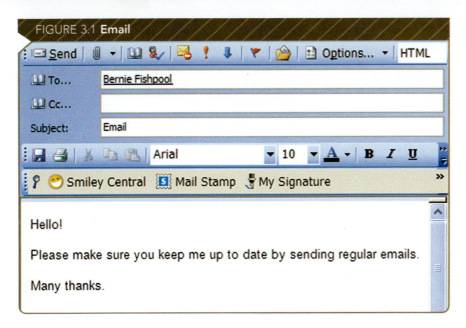

FIGURE 3.1 **Email**

Creating an account is easy and many of these services are free. Providers include Hotmail, Google and Yahoo amongst others.

### Text messaging

Text messaging is probably the simplest and most used of the communications media. Using a mobile phone, the sender creates a message by keying in each character using the telephone keypad.

Each press of a number will activate a letter. Take, for example, the number 8. Pressing this key once gives the letter T; twice gives the letter U and three times gives the letter V.

The message is sent by selecting the person to receive the message from the contacts list in the phone, or by keying in the number.

Once the message has been sent, it appears on the recipient's mobile phone. Text messages can be stored and viewed again.

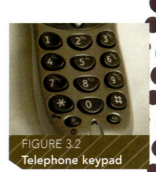

FIGURE 3.2
Telephone keypad

## Printed media

Printed media includes the following:

» newspapers and newsletters

» magazines

» reports

» brochures

» posters.

### Newspapers and newsletters

A newspaper is a multi-page publication that provides readers with a variety of information. National newspapers report on stories from anywhere in the world, but tend to focus mainly on things that happen in the UK. Local newspapers, on the other hand, tend to feature articles and stories about events in a much smaller, local area. Newspapers may be published daily or weekly.

Organisations sometimes create newsletters to communicate general information both to staff and to customers. A newsletter usually is made up of more than one page and contains information and articles of special interest.

Some newsletters are sent as paper copies, and some are sent electronically as documents attached to emails. Newsletters are published less frequently than newspapers; possibly only three or four times a year.

FIGURE 3.3 **Newsletter**

## Autumn Newsletter

Volume 1, Issue 1          November 2007

# BandStuff.com

**Staff profile - Chris**

Chris joined the company in the summer of 2007.

He completed his BTEC National Diploma and Higher National Diploma at a college in the west of England prior to starting work in the production section.

Chris is talented in graphics and has taken over as artistic supervisor choosing new logos, templates and layouts for a new range of

On holiday in Europe in the Autumn of 2007

Hoodies being introduced in January 08 (for full information see page 3).

Chris' hobbies include drawing and working with products like Blender to create 3D objects and animations.

Welcome to BandStuff.com Chris!

**Special points of interest:**

- New range of Hoodies available from January 08 (see page 3)

**Inside this issue:**

| | |
|---|---|
| Staff profile— | 1 |
| Band profile | 1 |
| New merchandise | 2 |
| Special offers | 3 |
| New returns policy | 4 |

**Band profile – Butterscotch Pudding**

Butterscotch Pudding have just released their first album on the Demon Bunny record label.

keyboard player Bekka.

The band has already been in the public eye for 3 years, playing

used as part of the backing track for the new role playing game **Conscious Choices** which is out on 8th

The example shown in Figure 3.2 is a company newsletter for BandStuff.com. Intended for staff and customers, it has information about a local band, a new member of staff and other articles to do with band merchandising.

JOIN IN

**Talk to your friends or classmates.**

How many examples of newspapers can you think of? Name some national and some local publications.

## Magazines

FIGURE 3.4 **Magazines**

Magazines tend to be themed and are targeted at a particular type of audience. For example, women's magazines tend to have articles about health, fashion and real-life case histories. However, car magazines are usually targeted at men and have articles about different types of car and new technologies.

Magazines are more likely to be published weekly or monthly and, as such, they are generally called periodicals (things published at regular intervals).

### Reports

Reports are formal multi-page documents used by organisations to present information about particular issues. Each year organisations publish financial reports that give a full breakdown of the organisation's financial health. They show the company's profit or loss and give an overview of what the company owns (for example, buildings, vehicles, stock, equipment). Financial reports are usually given to managers and stakeholders (people with an interest) in the organisation.

### Brochures

Brochures are similar to magazines but they are usually designed to sell something. The most familiar are holiday brochures. Holiday brochures contain information about different holiday destinations, general facts about resorts and information about places to stay and things to do.

FIGURE 3.5 **Travel brochures**

### Posters

A poster is a single-page document printed on one side only. Posters are usually large – not usually smaller than A4 size (standard white paper used in a printer). They are often used to advertise events, so will contain all the relevant information about the event such as:

» what the event is

» where it is being held (location)

» date and time

» ticket price (or if it is free)

» door opening time (particularly for a gig)

» any age restrictions.

The style of the poster will be suitable for the audience it is trying to attract. This includes which fonts (style of type) are used, any images and how the poster is laid out.

## Voice media

Voice media is based on the spoken word rather than the written word and includes the following:

» telephone

» face-to-face communication

» radio

» podcasts.

### Telephone

The mobile telephone is one of the biggest growth areas in technology for many reasons. The technology itself is becoming increasingly cheaper to produce and therefore more people can afford to own mobile phones. Additionally, the range of features that mobile phones have has expanded dramatically. The first mobile phone had few, if any, features – some maybe had the ability to store phone numbers or could be used as calculators.

Mobile phones now have the functionality to take pictures and video, record voice, play games and some are able to surf the net.

**FIND OUT**

On your way home from school or college, see if you can find three posters on public display.

Write down what they are for.

FIGURE 3.6
**Mobile with Internet connectivity**

### Face-to-face communication

Face-to-face communications is probably the most popular way of communicating and includes structured communications like interviews or meetings and unstructured conversations. However, getting people in the same room at the same time requires planning. Some people required to attend may have to travel to get to the meeting, so it can be time consuming and expensive.

### Radio

Radio is a one-way only transmission – you are not able to interact with either the device or the transmission, apart from a telephone call as part of a live broadcast. However, radio is still popular with many people. For example, people may prefer to listen to the news without seeing the often unpleasant images shown on TV. Radios are more portable than TVs and are an important part of communication in, for example, flight control and the emergency services.

### Podcasts

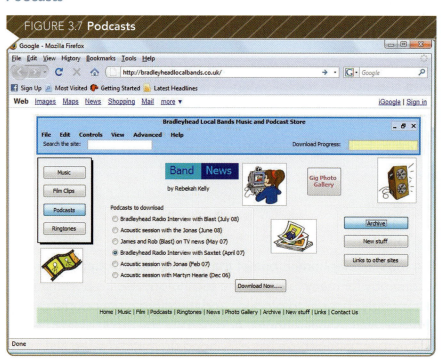

FIGURE 3.7 **Podcasts**

The Podcast is a recent technology using simple media files that can be downloaded to a device or computer and viewed at any time. Podcasts usually include moving image and sound.

The iTunes website has a range of podcasts, some of which you can download for free, others have to be paid for by subscription.

The different types of podcasts include:

» radio shows

» news items

» audio books.

Some podcasts also contain images such as:

» cartoons

» museum tours

» tutorials

» nature short films.

**TEAMWORK**

**Working with two or three others, identify and write down the names of five Internet websites where you can download podcasts. In each case, say whether the downloads are free or must be paid for.**

**Create a short PowerPoint presentation about podcasts. This should explain:**

**what they are**

**where they can be downloaded from.**

**LINKS**

## What is the business purpose of different types of communication?

There are three reasons why a business may want to communicate:

» to provide information, get a message across or educate

» to attract attention or persuade

» to entertain.

### Inform, get a message across or educate

User manuals for products are an example of a business communication designed to inform or get a message across. User manuals are usually designed and written with a very basic user in mind. More complex explanations and content will be presented as an advanced user manual.

### Attract attention or persuade

Posters, advertisements and flyers are designed to attract attention. Depending on the situation, businesses will use these to attract the interest of potential customers in their products or services.

Advertisements come in many shapes and sizes and may be paper-based or electronic. They can be displayed statically, such as advertisements in railway stations, or they may be shown on TV, video or DVD. They are used to promote events, goods or services to the public or to other businesses and are designed to attract as much attention as possible. Most companies have an advertising budget (an amount set aside each year for promotional or advertising activities).

THINK

**Think of three advertisements that you think attract attention.**

Compare your three with those of friends or colleagues. Decide why you think you have different answers.

**Write down the source of each advertisement, and the key points that you identified. Keep the research in your portfolio.**

LINKS

Flyers are usually used as a cheap method of advertising. They can be posted directly into people's letterboxes, placed under car windscreen wipers or simply handed to people passing by. Flyers can be used to advertise just about anything.

Well-written, well-presented advertisements and flyers are an excellent way of persuading people to at least look at your products and services.

### Entertain

Some businesses realise that advertisements are more memorable if the viewer is entertained by them. If people can remember the advert – and the product being advertised – the effects of advertising are more long-lasting. The risk of an amusing advertisement is that people remember the advertisement but not the product.

FIGURE 3.8 **Can you remember what this television advertisement was for?**

# Be able to use clear appropriate English and demonstrate numeracy skills in a range of simple business related communications

**B**usiness communications should always be presented professionally. On page 91, we will look at how you should check the spelling of the text in your documents and that facts are accurate. This may mean that you need to seek the help of others.

## Clear appropriate English

You are expected to use English that is appropriate for your audience, to write clearly and use the correct punctuation. This means that you have to select words carefully and check (proofread) what you write. It is usually better to use short, simple sentences so that everyone understands what you are tyring to say.

### Full stops and capitalisation
A capital letter (capitalisation) is used at the beginning of a sentence to show where it starts. The full stop is used to end sentences.

**DID YOU KNOW?**

Proofreading means reading your work carefully, checking for any errors so that they can be corrected before your work is seen by someone else.

The following is a paragraph with all the punctuation and capitalisation removed.

> you are expected to use English that is appropriate for your audience to write clearly and use the correct punctuation this means that you have to select words carefully and check proofread what you write it is usually better to use short simple sentences so that everyone understands what you are trying to say

When you read this paragraph, it is almost impossible to decide which bits go together. Using capital letters at the beginning of sentences and full stops at the end immediately helps!

### When do you use a comma in a sentence?

Commas are generally used:

1. to separate items in a list

2. when adding extra information to a sentence that is already complete without the extra information.

For example:

> The puppy was only three months old, and her name was Poppy.

We could have read the sentence without the words after the comma and the sentence would still have made sense.

> The puppy was only three months old.

The writer of the sentence needed to decide whether to add the detail about the puppy's name as the sentence would have been fine without it.

A comma is often used before the word 'but'. For example:

> "I said I would go, but I changed my mind."

### When, and how, do you use an apostrophe?

Many people find it difficult to use an apostrophe correctly. In general, apostrophes are most often used in two ways. The first is to show ownership (possession) of something. For example:

> Rebekah's dress (the dress owned by Rebekah)

> Mickey's car (the car owned by Mickey)

> A person's name (the name of a person)

Be warned, however, if the person's name ends in an 's' before it is made possessive (shows ownership of something). Then the apostrophe comes after the 's'. For example:

Mavis' glasses (the glasses owned by Mavis)

The boys' dog (the dog owned by more than one boy)

The other use of an apostrophe is to show that letters have been removed, usually when words are put together. For example:

It's going to rain. (It is going to rain.)

He doesn't come from Sweden. (He does not come from Sweden.)

THINK

**Try and put the apostrophes in the right places. Some are right and some are wrong. Can you tell which?**

I helped wash my Mums' car.

I wouldve' come if Id been invited.

How's your brother?

Don't forget that when using word processing software such as Microsoft Word, the program has a spelling and grammar checking facility that you can use to help you.

If the presentation and accuracy of a document is important and you are ever in any doubt about your spelling and grammar, then check with someone else. At school or college you can ask a fellow student or a teacher. In a work setting you can ask a colleague or a manager.

The presentation of information says something about its quality and professionalism and is particularly important in formal situations. This means checking spelling and grammar and thinking about how the document is laid out (how it looks).

Which of the two documents in Figure 3.9 is better?

When communicating by text through software such as Microsoft Word you can use the spell and grammar checking facilities to help you. Clearly, if there is no such facility, you need to do this yourself, or ask someone for help.

FIGURE 3.9 **Which version looks more professional?**

**A**

Dear Sir

With reference to your order, I can only apologise for the delay in sending you the outstanding items.

This has occurred as a result of production problems we have been experiencing.

Please be reassured, the remaining goods will be with you within the next three days.

Yours sincerely
The Manager

**B**

Dear Sr
With rEFerunce to your order, I can only apolgize for the delay in sending u the outstanding itms.
    This has occurred as A RESULt of producsion problems we have been experceng.

Please be reasured, the remaining goods will be with you wiThin the next three days.

Yours sincrley
    The Manager

Example A has no errors and is clearly laid out. Customers would have more confidence in an organisation that sent them Example A than one that sent them Example B.

### Sending a CV to a prospective employer

Would you ever consider sending a CV with multiple spelling errors to a prospective employer? If your answer to this question is yes, you should understand that you would be unlikely to get the job! You are unlikely to even get an interview. Employers want employees who can write clearly and who are willing to make a little extra effort for the organisation. This will not be the impression you give a prospective employer if your CV is full of errors.

You should remember that if you communicate as an employee with individuals outside the organisation, you are effectively representing that organisation.

JOININ

**How often do you proofread what you write?**

Proofread the text. in Figure 3.10. How many errors can you spot?

FIGURE 3.10 **How many errors can you spot?**

Manufacturing companys are organisations That make things that they cell as partly or completely finished products to other businesses or to individuals directly. They buy in the rore materials and then use there own staff and resources to turn the raw materials into finished goods. This will include organisations that manufacture things like food, clothing, funiture, paper products, chemicals, metal and electronic companents.

Some entire manufacturing prOCesses are now fully automated. One of the most well-known is in car manufacturing where robots build and process as much of the car infrastructure as possible, wilTth minimul human input.

## Numeracy skills

With the development of spreadsheets, it has become much easier to communicate information that involves numbers. The data in Figure 3.11 compares CD sales in northern and southern England in 2007 in each month.

FIGURE 3.11 **CD sales in northern and southern England in 2007**

|  | A | B | C |
|---|---|---|---|
| 1 | CD Sales 2007 | | |
| 2 | | North of England | Southern England |
| 3 | January | £2,551 | £2,654 |
| 4 | February | £1,875 | £3,788 |
| 5 | March | £1,934 | £1,241 |
| 6 | April | £2,378 | £1,879 |
| 7 | May | £3,451 | £1,804 |
| 8 | June | £3,524 | £1,897 |
| 9 | July | £2,789 | £2,164 |
| 10 | August | £1,972 | £2,297 |
| 11 | September | £1,968 | £3,154 |
| 12 | October | £1,714 | £1,997 |
| 13 | November | £2,351 | £2,654 |
| 14 | December | £1,082 | £2,333 |

Look at the data in Figure 3.10. Are you able to see easily whether sales have been higher in Northern or Southern England? Probably not, so let's look at this data represented as a simple graph.

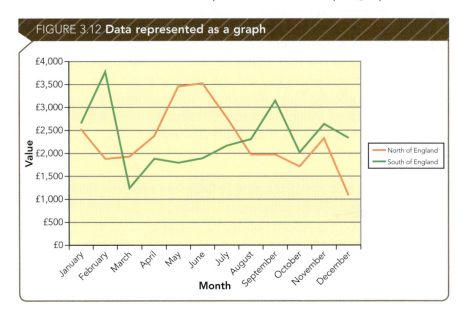

FIGURE 3.12 **Data represented as a graph**

Figure 3.12 more clearly shows that the North of England performed better than the South between March and July, but in the remainder of the year, the South performed better than the North. This type of graph is used to show trends, particularly when one year is compared to another year.

Charts and graphs are used to give a visual representation of numbers. They can be much easier to read than tables of values.

Look at the table of data in Figure 3.13.

FIGURE 3.13 **Fruit sales percentage data**

**Fruit Sales w/c 11th February 08**

|  | Totals | % Sales |
|---|---|---|
| Apples | 245 | 21 |
| Oranges | 365 | 32 |
| Pears | 210 | 18 |
| Melons | 188 | 16 |
| Berries | 142 | 12 |
| Total Sales | 1150 | |

The first thing to notice is that the sales of each fruit have been shown as a proportion of the total sales. This is done using a simple formula:

Single fruit total/Total sales x 100

However, even with the percentage of sales shown in the right-hand column, it is still difficult to visualise.

Let's look at what happens if you use the data from just the first and last columns and show it as a pie chart

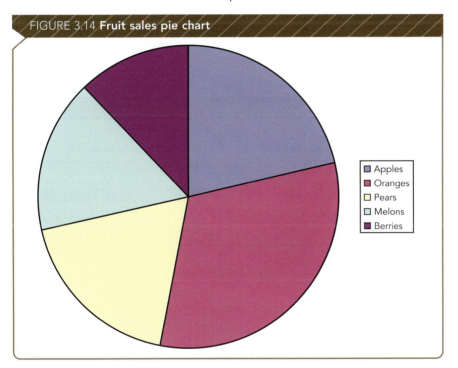

FIGURE 3.14 **Fruit sales pie chart**

- Apples
- Oranges
- Pears
- Melons
- Berries

Figure 3.14 makes it much clearer that oranges sold the most, followed in order by apples, pears, melons and berries. As can be seen, pie charts are excellent for establishing proportions of a whole. In this case, the pie chart shows how much of the total sales value was for each of the fruits.

If you need to compare columns of data, a column chart is more useful. Look at the table of data in Figure 3.15.

When the chart is created, the data is shown as coloured columns, with each colour representing a particular week.

This type of chart makes it much easier to compare information than reading a table of numbers.

Bar charts are similar to column charts and are also used to compare data, but the bars are displayed from left to right. Figure 3.17 uses the identical data to Figure 3.16.

FIGURE 3.15 **Weekly fruit sales data**

**Fruit Sales w/c 11th February 08 and w/c 18th February 08**

|  | Totals w/c 11th | Totals w/c 18th |
|---|---|---|
| Apples | 245 | 305 |
| Oranges | 365 | 291 |
| Pears | 210 | 177 |
| Melons | 188 | 216 |
| Berries | 142 | 182 |
| Total Sales | 1150 | 1171 |

FIGURE 3.16 **Weekly fruit sales column chart**

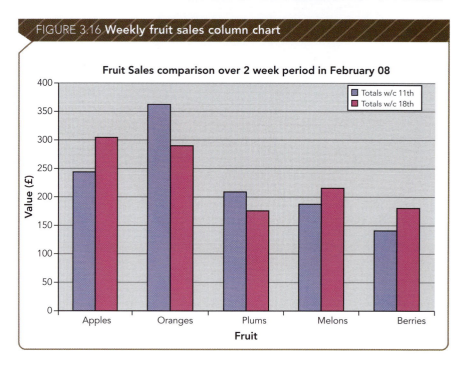

If you are creating charts or graphs to represent numeric information, you must use the right chart type to best display the data. Remember:

» pie charts are used to show values as a proportion of a whole

» column or bar charts are used to compare data

» line graphs are usually used to represent trends.

Whenever you work with numbers, charts and graphs you must check your work very carefully so that all calculations and graphical representations are correct.

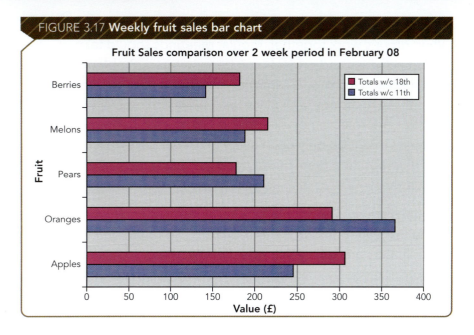

FIGURE 3.17 **Weekly fruit sales bar chart**

## Making text and numbers appropriate

When you write informally to friends or relatives, it is sometimes acceptable to use slang words or abbreviations. However, it is essential when writing business documents that they are written and laid out clearly to ensure that there are no misunderstandings about their content. Business documents should be proofread before being sent to ensure that the spelling and grammar is correct and any numbers used are accurate.

**In a work setting, you are representing the organisation – you must make sure that their reputation is maintained by producing written documentation of a high standard.**

You need to think about who you are communicating with – you can be more informal when communicating with friends and relatives.

## How organisations communicate verbally

In general, organisations communicate verbally through:

» meetings

» telephone

» presentations.

### Meetings

When groups work together, regular meetings should take place so that activities and projects can be monitored. Problems can be identified and the group can work together to find solutions. How often these meetings take place will be determined by the specific activities or projects. For example, if not much is happening, meetings might be only once every two weeks. However, if there is a lot going on, the team might need to have weekly or even daily meetings.

Meetings are an opportunity to check progress and make sure that all the tasks are being done as required, and to the deadline set for them. If tasks are falling behind schedule, the group can reallocate or reorder tasks. By sharing some of the work to help the individual responsible for doing the task, it is much more likely to be done on time and to the standard required.

Using webcams and other video technologies, it is increasingly possible to run conferences or meetings without needing everyone to be physically present.

Meetings usually take place in the work setting and they can often be relatively informal. For example, a departmental meeting about health and safety might be called so that proposed improvements can be shared with all members of the department. A specialist might be invited to give advice to the group, or they could do this via a webcam link rather than attending in person.

A conference is a more formal type of meeting where invited speakers present a specific item or information to the group.

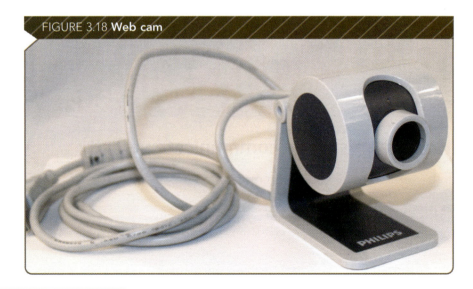

FIGURE 3.18 **Web cam**

Those not attending the conference may be present via a video link, watching the presentation on a large screen. Or the speaker might be linked into the conference. With the use of microphones and webcam or video technology, this process can also be fully interactive.

## Telephone messages

It is essential to take details about a telephone message as accurately as possible. For example, let's imagine that you have been told that Jane called, but you are not told when she called, you don't know which Jane it was and you don't know what it was about. In this situation you have no idea who to call back.

It is a good idea to use some sort of message pad or form like the one in Figure 3.19 to make sure you ask for the right information.

FIGURE 3.19 **Telephone message form**

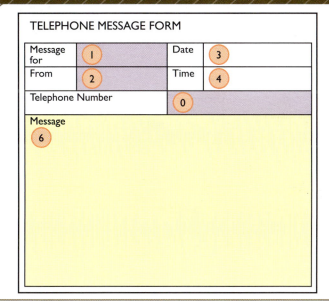

Checklist

1) The name of the person the message is for.

2) The name of the person the message is from.

3) Date the person called.

4) Time the person called.

5) Telephone number of the person calling (so that the person the message is for can call them back).

6) The content of the message. Try and make sure that the information you write down is clear and complete.

**THINK**

Create your own telephone message template. Print out five copies and take them home.

Answer your home phone five times for members of your family and take messages using the template you created. Each time you do this, discuss with the person the message is for how effective you were in taking messages for them. Did you improve your technique each time you took a message?

Keep the used message forms in your portfolio. Write a short explanation of what you did to improve your technique.

LINKS

### Presentations

Presentations normally use a combination of digital and verbal tools. For example, it is unlikely that a presenter would simply run a PowerPoint presentation and expect the audience to read it. It is more likely that they will talk alongside the presentation and be available to answer questions.

When presenting information, you need to prepare carefully. You should run through your presentation in full, at least once to practise your timings, before presenting it to your audience. You will be more familiar with the material and better able to present clearly both the information and your views.

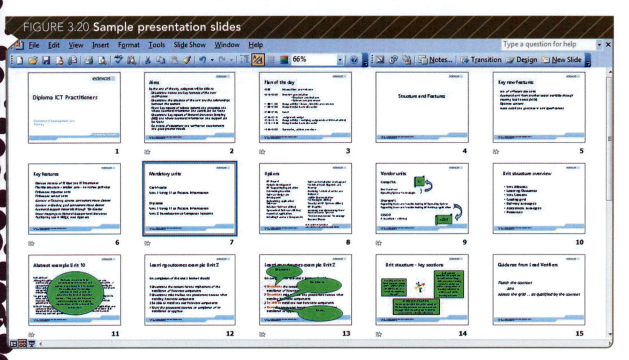

FIGURE 3.20 **Sample presentation slides**

The text and images should have been checked thoroughly for:

» completeness

» accuracy

» typos

» grammatical errors.

The organisation you represent will be judged on the quality of its presented communications. Poor presentation might be seen as representing a poor organisation. A smart and professional presentation is likely to be seen as representing a smart and professional organisation.

Whether giving a formal presentation or preparing to create a document, it is essential that you consider carefully in advance what you are going to say and how you are going to say it. A professional impression is created by writing and speaking clearly, and using language appropriate to the situation. Slang expressions and abbreviations should be avoided. The problem with using slang and abbreviations is that they may not be understood in the way intended.

For example, if I told you this book was wicked, what would you understand? In slang terms, this probably means it is a really good book. But the original meaning would be that the book was evil or morally wrong.

**FIND OUT**

See if you can think of three or four more words, or phrases, like 'wicked', that can be easily misunderstood. Check by trying them out on your friends and relatives.

## How organisations communicate in writing

Written forms of communication include:

» letters

» reports

» email

» web pages.

### Letters

Letters are a formal method of communication and usually arrive at their destination through a postal system such as the Royal Mail. Even though they might have been created and stored electronically, the actual letter will have been printed, put in an addressed envelope, stamped or franked and sent through a postal system. Business letters are usually printed on letterhead paper – paper that has the organisation's details printed on it, usually at the top.

### Reports

Reports, as mentioned on page 84, are multi-page documents used by organisations to record and present information around particular issues. For example, the sales team at BandStuff.com might write a report that gives managers information about the sales activities over the last two years, or the distribution staff might provide a report about distribution problems that have been experienced over the last three months. Sometimes reports are used to document the results of research.

FIGURE 3.21 **Report pages**

| Title of Report

Name of writer | Contents | Introduction | Page 3 / Page 2 / Page 1 of Report | Conclusions | Appendices and Bibliography (if appropriate) |

A report usually contains some or all of the following features:

» a front page showing the **title** of the report and the name of the person who wrote it

» a list of the **contents**, showing page numbers as appropriate

» an **introduction** that explains what the report is about

» the **main body**, which contains the information the report is seeking to communicate

» **conclusions**, which will bring the report to a close

» sometimes the report concludes with **recommendations**, for any changes that might need to be made

» **appendices** may be added

» the report might end with a **bibliography** – a list of sources used in the preparation of the report.

### Email

Email is a short way to say electronic mail, a form of written communication sent and received via a computer.

The advantages of emails are:

» They are quick. The person receiving the email may receive it within seconds of it being sent.

» Emails can be any length from a few words or lines to a number of pages.

» They can contain both text and images.

» They can be sent with attachments.

» They don't cost anything extra – you are already paying for the service by paying your provider for connection to the Internet.

## Web pages

Web pages are to a website what pages are to a book. Websites contain a number of web pages (individual screens) that are linked together.

The website is accessed through a web address, also known as a URL.

To access the website shown in Figure 3.22 we have three options.

FIGURE 3.22 **Pearson Education website**

**Option 1** is to find the Pearson Education website through a search engine such as Google. Once you have accessed the main page, you then click on the relevant links until you find the page you want.

**Option 2** is to type the address of the company's home page into a web browser, for example:

www.pearson.com

This will take you to the home page and you then, as in option 1, have to find the page you want using links.

**Option 3** is when you have the exact address of the page you want to access. In this case, you key this into the web browser and the page you want will be immediately available. The following address takes us directly to the Pearson Education website:

http://www.pearson.com/index.cfm?pageid=18

Clearly this longer address is difficult to remember which is why you have the option to bookmark (save the URL) of any pages you might want to use frequently, or need to go back to for your research.

## Know how behaviour, personal styles and actions affect communication and achievement of objectives

**B**oth in your work and your personal life, how you behave is generally a reflection of who you are. At work, you represent the organisation you work for and you should always try to make a good impression by being polite and professional. To do this, you need to be aware of your personal style.

There may be times in your life when your personal style changes. For example, when you are with your family or friends you probably behave differently compared to when you are at work, or in a more formal environment.

When it comes to working with other people, your style should always be the same – considerate, fair, honest and professional.

**THINK**

Think about yourself. What do you think the way that you behave and your personal style say about you? Identify one thing that you think is good and one thing about you that you think is less good and discuss with a teacher/tutor.

# Personal styles

You are in control of the style that you choose to adopt. The following are examples of a range of personal styles and situations where a particular style might be appropriate.

### Professional/unprofessional

Being professional means that you set yourself high standards in what you say, in what you do and in how you present yourself. In general, professional people are helpful, organised and positive.

People who are unprofessional are often obstructive, disorganised and negative.

### Helpful/obstructive

Being helpful means doing as much as possible to make sure that tasks are completed to a high standard. It often means doing more than is asked for. It also means being generous with time and skills - even when it is of no personal benefit.

Being obstructive means doing as little as possible and not volunteering help. It also means not completing tasks, doing them badly or carelessly and blaming others when things don't get done.

### Organised/disorganised

Organised people are creative, neat and tidy. They do tasks with care and effort and give the impression of commitment.

Disorganised people usually appear to lack commitment. They are often untidy and show less effort and care in their work.

### Positive/negative

Being positive or negative can be communicated by facial expressions and body language. It is also communicated both by the words people choose and the way in which they use them.

Positive people tend to smile a lot and are usually considerate and courteous to other people. They will choose words carefully to create a positive feeling in others.

Negative people tend to frown and may look unhappy or angry. They are often self-centred and withdrawn and use words that make other people also feel negative.

**DID YOU KNOW?**

Positive words include: good, great, excellent, interesting, keen, proud, pleasing, safe, rewarding, yes.

Negative words include: Wrong, inappropriate, against, contrary, less, minus, opposed, problematic, no.

FIGURE 3.23
**Smiling**

FIGURE 3.24
**Crying**

FIGURE 3.25
**Angry face**

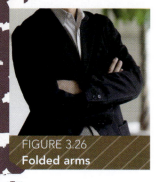
FIGURE 3.26
**Folded arms**

## Body language

Body language communicates as much about what a person is feeling or thinking as their words do.

The following are examples of body language and what they might mean.

A smile may be an indication that someone is happy. It is difficult to smile when you are feeling angry or sad.

Although crying is usually considered a strong sign that someone is feeling very sad, it is the down-turned mouth that is really the indicator of sadness. Remember, some people cry when they are very happy or something good has happened to them!

It may be clear from the facial expression that the person is angry. However, angry people also often shout and gesticulate (wave their arms around in an angry or threatening way).

Many people believe that if someone folds their arms they are putting a barrier between them and the person they are speaking to. Folded arms are often associated with people being angry.

Shouting is not necessarily an indication of anger. It depends on what the person is shouting, the tone of voice they are using and the words they are shouting. Shouting may be used as a warning to alert another person that they are in danger. You might also shout to attract attention if you are in danger yourself.

With experience, it is often easy to spot how people are feeling based on their facial expressions and their body language.

## Speed and quality of work

Some people think that it is best to complete your work quickly. However, the faster work is completed, the more possibility there is for errors to be made. For this reason, others think that to ensure work is of good quality, it should be done slowly.

In fact, the key to producing high quality work is to work as quickly as you can, but also keep checking that you haven't made any mistakes. It is always a good idea to check your work again once it is complete.

# Personality types

Your personal style is something over which you have some choice and control. However, people are sometimes classified by their personality type. For example, some people like to be leaders. They like to influence what takes place. Other people like to follow – they like to be told what to do and how to do it. Your personality type is likely to be something that has developed over a number of years and may be more difficult to change.

The following are examples of personality types that have been identified in teams. Each of the roles described is important to the team's success.

### Leader

The team leader needs to be calm under pressure, patient with team members and willing to take calculated risks to ensure the team's success. Team leaders will: take decisions; encourage team members to participate; keep the team on track and resolve disagreements.

### Ideas person

The ideas person needs to be enthusiastic and not afraid to experiment. Ideas people will be able to: think of new and original ideas; think of different ways of doing things and come up with solutions to problems.

### Peacemaker or compromiser

The peacemaker or compromiser is the person in the team who will always seek to find a resolution to conflict. The peacemaker will try and find the middle ground between two opposing points of view and help reach a solution that both sides can accept.

# Effective communication and performance

Applying what you have learned in this unit will help you to do your job well, to achieve your goals and deadlines and make you an effective communicator. It will assist you in achieving your personal objectives and help others to achieve theirs.

# Be able to work in a team to meet agreed objectives, demonstrating active listening skills and effective confident speaking skills

**A** team is a collection of people, like those shown in Figure 3.26, who work together for a specific reason.

## Working in a team

To work effectively teams must:

» agree objectives and have clear goals

» have good lines of communication

» listen to each other and compromise when necessary

» plan tasks well and execute them (carry them out) as a team.

## Agree objectives and have clear goals

Objectives should be set out clearly and explained fully. They should be written and kept as a permanent record that can be referred to at a later date. It is essential for a team's success that each team member fully understands the objectives.

As a minimum, the team should agree:

» what must be done

» for whom

» by when.

A team that does not have clear goals is likely to fail in its objectives. Everyone in the team should know the end product or goal that they are trying to achieve. For example, a team might be aiming to sell a certain number of products, or maybe to publish a book at a certain time. If everyone in the team knows and understands what the team is trying to achieve, they are more likely to pull in the same direction.

## Have good lines of communication

Teams need good communication skills to exchange ideas and to give and receive instructions.

For example, a rowing team needs to row so that the oars do not bang into each other. It makes the action smoother and helps to improve the speed of the boat.

FIGURE 3.27
A rowing team

Teams must be prepared to work collaboratively (together), helping each other with tasks if needed. A good team member is not trying to prove how good they are as an individual, but how well they can help the team to achieve its objectives.

**TEAMWORK**

**Together with three friends or classmates, research and develop a PowerPoint presentation about 'good communication skills'.**

You need to organise yourselves as a team. You should agree the tasks that need to be done, decide who will do each task, agree how the work will be presented and create the finished PowerPoint slide show.

Deliver the presentation to a group of classmates or to your teacher/tutor.

**Write a short description of three key things you feel you learned from this exercise.**

**Keep the presentation and your written description in your portfolio.**

**LINKS**

### Listening skills and compromise

Working as part of a team requires individuals to develop good listening skills (see pages 111–12).

This is for two reasons:

» First, you need to listen to ensure that you have a full understanding of what the other person is saying.

» Second, if you constantly talk, people who are less confident won't have an opportunity to speak. Their views and ideas are equally important to the team.

There will be times when, in order to move forward, team members will have to compromise to reach an agreement. A compromise is needed when both parties have very strong and good reasons for wanting to take a particular course of action. The compromise will be the solution that both parties will accept and might be made by using aspects of both viewpoints. It might not be ideal, but will resolve the situation.

For example, when planning a conference, one team member

considers that the venue should be small, accommodating between 50 and 70 people. However, another team member thinks that the venue should be large, accommodating 200 plus. After talking it through as a team, a compromise is reached and a venue suitable for a group size of 130 to 160 is booked.

There will be situations where a compromise cannot be reached. At these times you should remember that working as a team means showing fairness and consideration to others. It is not good teamwork to force ideas on other team members. If a resolution cannot be reached, the team will need to ask an independent (non-team member) person to help. For example, in school you could ask a teacher/tutor or at work you could ask a manager.

### Make a plan and execute it

The team needs a plan to achieve its agreed goals.

Part of planning is to give each team member roles and responsibilities, making sure that everyone is clear about what they need to do. A permanent, written record of the tasks allocated is also an essential part of a formal team plan. This record can be referred to at a later date if people have forgotten or are unsure of what their roles and responsibilities involve.

If there is no written record, there may be confusion about the team's objectives and how they are going to achieve them. Time will be wasted trying to renegotiate goals and eventually may mean that nothing at all is achieved.

When planning, the team will also have to agree about the way in which tasks are carried out. For example, to carry out market research the team may decide to use a questionnaire to interview potential customers. If this is for an important project, the team may decide to engage an outside agency to carry out this research.

During the planning period, team members must work cooperatively. However, remember that individual team members may not agree all of the time. Each person has different views and experiences that need to be taken into account when negotiating how things should be done.

When disagreement occurs, the situation must be handled carefully and must be resolved. Failure to do this may mean that individuals lose motivation and commitment to the project. In this situation, the team is unlikely to acheive its objectives.

CHECK IT OUT

Software is available to help create and keep track of a project plan. Visit http://office.microsoft.com and see what you can find out about Microsoft Office project 2007.

Team communications should be clear to make sure that it is not possible to misunderstand what has been said or planned. The team is likely to hold regular meetings to make sure that tasks are kept on course as the plan is carried out. Meetings give team members the opportunity to track progress and offer support to each other.

Team meetings should have a positive focus. The team leader will probably also act as a chairperson for the team and should direct discussions about any issues on which the team can't agree. It is important that the team discuss these areas without getting emotional. The team should be comfortable with any agreement reached to resolve the problem. (See pages 109–10.)

Working as a team means supporting other team members, not letting them down and taking equal responsibility for things that go wrong: for example, when deadlines are missed, or the work produced is not of the right quality or the product is not what was originally promised. If someone has let them down, individual team members should not be asked to do more work than they expected to. In this case, the team leader should decide who else in the team can help by taking on some of the extra work required. In this way, the team's objectives will be reached more efficiently.

## Active listening skills

One of the most difficult skills to master is the art of effective listening. There are two main attributes:

» The ability to listen without interrupting.

» The ability to listen and respond appropriately to what was said.

### The ability to listen without interrupting

It is polite to listen without interrupting. This is true not just when taking part in a group activity, but also when having a one-to-one conversation with someone.

Sometimes it is very difficult to listen without butting in, especially if you feel strongly about something. However, interrupting to express your own point of view may seem rude and that you are not listening to the speaker. It could trigger an argument.

Disagreements can be useful because they allow individuals to share opposing views and at times this allows new ideas to be introduced. However, disagreements must be handled carefully because arguments can be very destructive.

### Listening to ensure that you can respond appropriately to others

Good listening skills make you an effective and useful team member.

If you do not listen carefully in a particular situation, how can you be sure that your response is appropriate? Have you ever, for example, answered a question in class only then to realise that you'd not heard the question properly and you'd given an inappropriate answer?

Listening carefully gives you clues about how you should respond and ensures that you give the right answer. For example, if somebody tells you that their best friend has just died, it would be unfortunate and hurtful if you responded with a smile or a laugh.

## Effective, confident speaking skills

Most people, even well-known public speakers, get nervous when they speak in front of others. For some, it depends on how many people are in the audience, or for others, it can be what they are speaking about or the location that makes them nervous. Either way, it tends to get easier with practice.

### Make relevant contributions to discussions

Speaking confidently is easier when you feel that you are making good contributions. What you say during a discussion should be logical and should fit in with the issues being discussed.

### Present information and views clearly and in appropriate language

Think about what you are going to say before you say it! Make sure you have time to plan and prepare if you are presenting to other people. There may be times when your audience disagrees with you – even so, you are entitled to share your thoughts.

Try and speak clearly and slowly. It is expected that you will use language at a level that is appropriate to your audience. For example, if you are presenting something very technical, you might need to find easier words that non-technical people will be able to understand.

FIGURE 3.28
**Speaking confidently**

JOIN IN

**Create a three-minute presentation about your favourite computer game.**

Practise the presentation in front of three different people (e.g., a teacher/tutor, a family member, a friend).

Ask for their feedback. How do they think the presentation went? What do they think you could improve on?

Each time, see if you can use their suggestions to make improvements.

# Be able to reflect on the workings of teams and the different roles individuals play within teams, demonstrating self awareness

**A**t the end of a team project, it is important that you reflect on how the team worked together so that you can learn from your experiences. Sometimes it is useful to reflect with other members of the team – sometimes it is equally useful to think about these issues alone, or with a teacher/tutor or supervisor.

You should think about:

» **What went well** – identify tasks that were completed successfully and decide why this was the case.

» **What went badly** – identify tasks that were not completed successfully and decide why this was the case.

» **How effective the team was** – think about whether the team worked well together and if so why, or if not, what the problems were.

» **Personality mix** – look at the personality types in the group. Did you have too many trying to be leaders, or not enough ideas people?

» **Contribution of individuals** – did all team members contribute equally? If not, identify why not. It is not acceptable for one or two team members to do all the work and for the rest to do nothing.

» **Feedback from a reviewer (someone outside the team)** – you will usually receive feedback on a team project either from a client or a manager. This should be taken into account as it is often true that an outsider can observe things that people in the team miss.

## Self awareness

Throughout your life, other people will tell you things about you. Your family may tell you that you are noisy, naughty, good, considerate, inconsiderate, selfish or honest, and so on. Your teachers may tell you that you are good at some subjects but not so good at others. You may have been told you that you work well as part of a team, or that you work better alone, that you have leadership skills, or that you are reliable or honest.

As you grow older, you will be expected to identify some of these behaviours or qualities in yourself. This is known as self awareness. You may ask others to help you with this process, but ultimately it is what you think about yourself that is important.

You should be able to identify your strengths, such as:

» what you are good at

» what skills you have

» what abilities you have

» what your preferences are.

You should be able to identify your weaknesses, such as:

» what you are not good at

» what skills you feel you lack

» what you are not able to do

» what you dislike.

This will help you to identify any skills you need to gain and any weaknesses you need to overcome.

If you have developed a sense of self awareness, you will be happy to receive feedback from others because facing your strengths and weaknesses will help you to learn. You will be able to evaluate your own performance and understand how your own behaviour has affected the performance of the team. It is important for your own development that you reflect in a completely honest way.

### Skills audit

A skills audit is a list of things you think you can do (strengths) or can't do (weaknesses). Try and identify **at least 10** of each and produce a table to display the information.

Discuss your strengths, skills and weaknesses with your teacher/tutor.

Create a plan for how you think you might improve on at least one of your weaknesses.

**LINKS**

When you are on your work experience, take time to observe your colleagues. Identify **one** thing about each of your colleagues that you think is a good example of their professionalism.

At the end of your work experience, ask your manager to identify **three** examples of ways in which you behaved professionally.

# ... a web developer

**Name:** Robert Bennett

**Age:** 27 years

**Employer:** An online travel company

» **Roles and responsibilities (what I do in my job as a web developer):**

Working in a small team, we build the web pages and templates for the whole website. I maintain and update existing web pages and templates.

I have to make sure that all the programming codes I use are correct; otherwise the website will not work correctly.

» **Qualifications:**

3 A-levels
A degree in Computing
A masters degree in Multimedia and the Internet

» **What I like about my job:**

I enjoy the environment of an online/media company – it's much more relaxed than the other industries seem to be. Technologies in the industry are continuously changing, allowing you to grow and develop within your job. Dealing with web technologies is always a challenge as you are constantly learning the new techniques or pieces of software, so you're constantly updating your skills and learning something new almost every week, which helps keep the job interesting.

I also like working for a big company which is worldwide as often it means I can travel.

The people who work within the web industry are always very relaxed so the team I work with get on very well and we always help one another if we're busy. It's great to know that if I have a problem, there's always someone to go to.

» **The hardest part of my job:**

Due to the nature of the travel industry we need to constantly update our website and try to come up with new, innovative ways to sell holidays. Obviously, the new ideas come from a different team from mine, so there are always lots of different people to try and keep happy.

Sometimes, when we have a big deadline coming up, I have to work long hours to get everything done. I do think it's worth it though when you see all your work go live on the website!

✳ Robert Bennett

# Case Study

## BandStuff.com →

Whilst on work experience at Bandstuff.com you realise that the company has problems with its internal communications.

You have been asked to work as part of a team to create an A3 poster. This poster will be displayed around the company to provide information, advice and guidance on the key points of effective communication.

As a team, you must agree on the objectives of this activity and set deadlines for tasks. You should draw up a team plan and allocate roles and responsibilities. Next, you must execute the plan, keeping track of progress. Lastly, you will create a draft poster.

## Questions

1. Did you work well as a team? What went well, and why? What went less well, and why?

2. Did you achieve your objectives? Was this in the timeframe you had set? If not, why?

3. If you had to do this project again, what would you do differently?

For this unit you will need to present a portfolio which will be a combination of coursework assignments, classwork and activities. Your teacher will award marks for the work you have submitted across three mark bands.

## Task One: Effective communication

You will be given an assignment that asks you to investigate different communication media and comment on the three main types of media and their uses, placing them in a business context.

You will also need to show that you can produce some business communications that provide textual and numerical information.

To prepare for this assessment, think about the following, find some examples that you can use to guide you and make some notes:

» Types of communication media (finding as many examples as possible of each type).

» Carefully investigate each one and decide whether you think it is a good example and make a list of good points you see. Make a second list of what is bad under the title 'What to avoid'.

## Task Two: Team challenge

You will also be expected to work on a group project where you will plan and execute a task.

» Make sure you know your own strengths and weaknesses so that when you are put into your group you can share this information with the team.

» Make a list of your skills such as word processing or research.

» Be aware of your personality type and be prepared to share this information with the team.

» Create a simple diary/logbook where you can write down how the team is working together as you do the assessment so that you have a record you can draw on when you reflect on your own performance and the performance of others.

# SUMMARY / SKILLS CHECK

» **Communicate effectively and clearly**

✓ This unit has introduced you to the concepts of effective communication and has highlighted the tools available to support you in making your communications effective and professional.

✓ One of the commonest ways that organisations communicate is in writing. This has been made easier through growth in technology systems, such as word processing and email. The tools now embedded in these systems, such as spellchecking and grammar checking, enable everyone to improve the quality of their written English. Similarly, numerical packages make it possible to communicate complex numerical information through the use of charts and graphs.

✓ Listening and speaking are essential skills for an effective employee. You will develop your own skills in these areas through message taking and giving presentations.

» **Develop a personal style and behave in a way that has a positive effect on the achievement of objectives**

✓ Your personal style says a lot about who you are. Through this unit you have gained an understanding about developing your personal style and behaviour, and how these can make you more successful in a positive way both in achieving your own goals and those of your team.

» **Work as part of a team**

✓ Unless you choose to be self-employed, you are likely to work as part of a team. This team could be small with one or two other people, or could be quite large – with maybe ten or more individuals working together.

✓ You have been introduced to basic principles of teamwork and should now understand the behaviours and attitudes needed to promote good working relationships. Listening and contributing in a positive way helps you to achieve your own objectives and also makes you a more effective team member.

» **Evaluate your own contributions to a team and as an individual**

✓ It is relatively easy to find positive and negative things to say about people you work with. It can, however, be difficult to reflect honestly about your own performance. Through this unit you have gained a number of techniques to help you evaluate and reflect in a constructive (positive and useful) way.

# OVERVIEW

This is a practical, hands-on unit through which you will learn about the key components of network systems such as workstations, network interfaces, switches and cabling, printers and network drives.

You will also learn about how PC systems can be networked in different ways, how to connect at least one PC to an existing network and how to test the functionality of the network. This includes finding out how to resolve simple networking problems such as missing or out of date print drivers, simple connection issues and mapping a drive.

Ideally, you will learn about different components by handling them and finding out what each one does. To start with, you will probably do this by looking at components taken from computers that are no longer being used. Once you are familiar with the components and their function (what they do), you will be allowed to look at them in working computers linked to networks.

# 04

# Network Systems

## Skills list

At the end of this unit, you should:

» Know how a PC is connected to a network

» Be able to connect a PC to an existing network and resolve simple problems

## Job watch

Some jobs that make use of these skills include:

» help desk assistant
» network engineer
» computer salesperson.

# Know how a PC is connected to a network

To connect a PC to a network you first have to collect all the resources you will need. This will include various pieces of hardware (devices you can see and touch) and software (instructions that make the hardware work).

The IT systems you work with at school or college tend to be PCs that are connected to a network, but the actual components used may vary.

Let's take a look at the workstation resources required.

### Workstation (hardware)

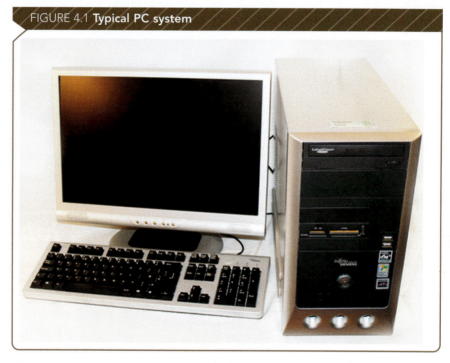

FIGURE 4.1 **Typical PC system**

The workstation is the name commonly used to describe a PC when it is connected to a network. The user interacts with the workstation using a keyboard and mouse.

The workstation output is typically shown on a monitor screen.

A workstation has many components, such as:

» case

» PSU (power supply unit)

» motherboard

» processor (or CPU – central processing unit)

» RAM (random access memory)

» hard disk

» graphics card

» sound card

» optical drive, e.g. CD (compact disc) or DVD (digital versatile disk).

### Wired network card (hardware)

FIGURE 4.2 **Wired network card**

This is often referred to as a NIC (network interface card). It plugs into the motherboard and can send and receive network data over an Ethernet cable.

Workstations are said to be 'integrated' when the NIC is built into the motherboard.

### Wireless network card (hardware)
A popular alternative to wired network cards is the use of a wireless card.

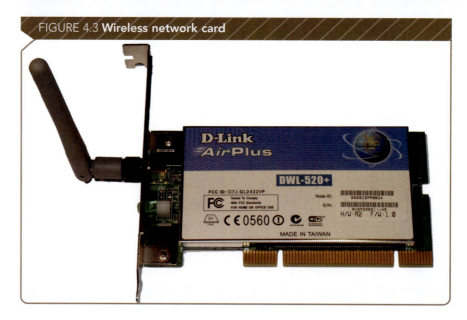

FIGURE 4.3 **Wireless network card**

Wireless networks (often shortened to 'Wi-Fi') use radio waves to send and receive network data.

Wireless cards can also be plugged into a workstation motherboard, or may integrated.

### USB wireless adaptor (hardware)

You may be familiar with USB (Universal Serial Bus) connections from devices such as MP3 players, flash drives and game consoles.

It is also possible to buy small, portable wireless adaptors that fit into a PC's USB socket. These are often easier to use than installing wireless cards.

FIGURE 4.4 **USB wireless adaptor**

### Operating systems (software)

FIGURE 4.5 **Windows Vista**

Operating systems control the hardware and support the running of applications. They provide an interface for the user to 'talk to' the hardware and allow the hardware to talk back to the user, informing them of any errors encountered.

Most PCs have Microsoft Windows operating systems – for example, XP or Vista – installed. However, other systems, such as Linux, may be used instead.

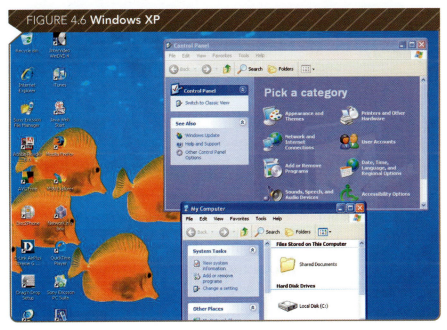

FIGURE 4.6 **Windows XP**

Windows has a user-friendly 'point + click' interface.

All recent operating systems have built-in network support and drivers to help the operating system 'talk' to the hardware; for example, a network card.

In addition to the PC workstations, it is necessary to have the correct equipment for the required connections. This is called the network infrastructure.

Let's take a look at these components in more detail.

### Switch or hub (hardware)

These are electronic devices that share network communication with connected devices. A switch is more effective than a hub at managing network traffic.

FIGURE 4.7
**Network switch**

### Ethernet cable or wireless connection (hardware)

We've already seen that workstations may be connected to a network by wired Ethernet cables, or by wireless radio waves.

Ethernet cables are sometimes called Cat5 (Category 5). Wireless is popular but less secure and signals can be weakened by distance and interference.

## Wireless base station (hardware)

FIGURE 4.9 **Wireless base station**

FIGURE 4.8
**Ethernet cable**

**CHECK IT OUT**

Visit www.btbroadband information.com and click on the 'Glossary' tab. You will find many useful definitions there, including Cat 5, Ethernet cable, hub, optical cable and Wi-Fi.

This is also sometimes known as a WAP (wireless access point).

Some base stations are also routers. Routers are used to connect to an ISP (internet services provider) for access to the World Wide Web (WWW) and other online services.

**ASK**

**Identify whether your school or college has the correct workstation resources and network infrastructure to connect two or more PC workstations together.**

Create a checklist of the hardware and software components in each workstation, and the type of network infrastructure that may be used.

How many did you find and recognise? Are all the required components there?

**Compare your list with that of another class member and create a combined final version of the list.**
**Place the list in your portfolio.**

**LINKS**

## Networked PC systems

Technology systems are useful when they 'stand alone'. However, better use can be made of them when they are connected together to form a network. This allows users to share common resources such as printers and network drives. It also offers opportunities for improved communication through electronic mail and the Internet.

Networks can be connected into two basic configurations – either wired (using an Ethernet cable) or wirelessly (using Wi-Fi).

These two configurations are called peer-to-peer and client-server.

Most organisations have networks that help them to operate their business successfully and make their employees more productive.

On your work experience, find out what type of network is being used by the organisation you are visiting. How does the network compare to the one you use in school or college?

### Simple networks

A simple wired networked PC system can be formed by connecting two PCs together using two network cards, one switch and two Ethernet cables.

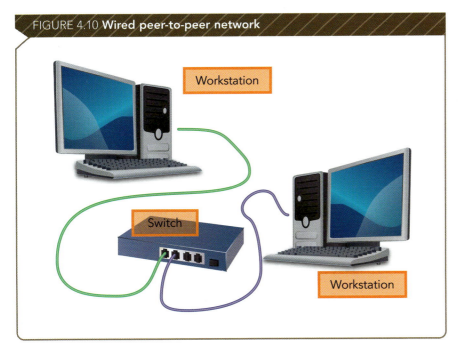

FIGURE 4.10 **Wired peer-to-peer network**

This is a peer-to-peer system. Both PCs are called 'peers' because each workstation shares the same level of importance and responsibility for running and maintaining the network. Usually this means that each workstation will be able to share the network resources, such as printers and network drives, of the other.

Let's examine an example of a wireless peer-to-peer network.

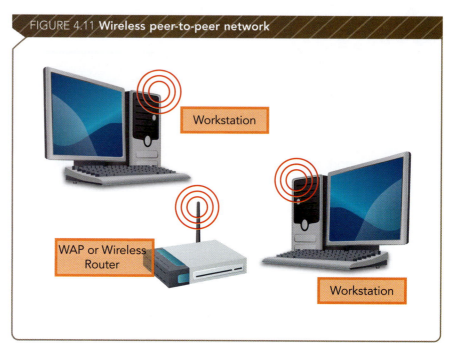

FIGURE 4.11 **Wireless peer-to-peer network**

Workstation

WAP or Wireless Router

Workstation

Peer-to-peer systems may also use a wireless infrastructure consisting of two PC workstations (each with wireless adapter) and one wireless base station (WAP or wireless router). This is the most common type of LAN (local area network) used in the home and small offices.

Wireless connections allow more flexibility in how workstations are positioned as there are no Ethernet cables to worry about. In addition, unlike an infrared TV remote control, Wi-Fi signals can travel further and even pass through solid walls.

As we will see, wireless networks are a little more complex to setup and test.

Now let's turn our attention to client-server networks.

A server is usually a more powerful PC system that is in charge of network traffic resources such as printing and files, and in some cases may even perform some of the client workstation's processing.

Servers require a different version of an operating system to manage a network effectively. For Microsoft Windows, the current

FIGURE 4.12 **Wired client-server network**

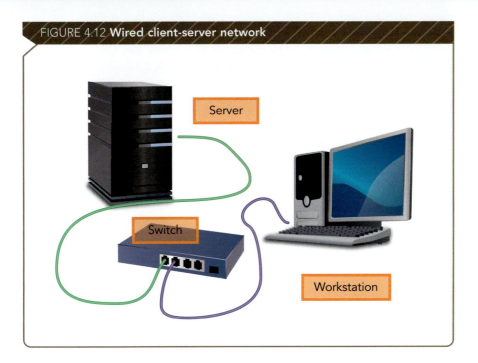

server version is Windows Server 2008, although Windows Server 2003 is still popular.

We can set up a similar network using wireless technology.

FIGURE 4.13 **Wireless client-server network**

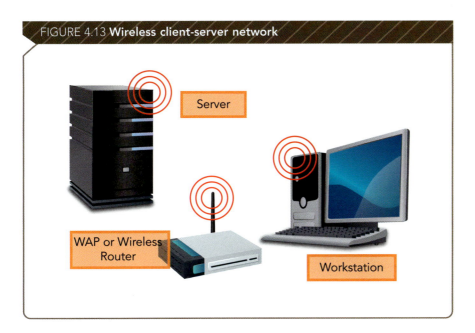

# Be able to connect a PC to an existing network and resolve simple problems

**N**ow that you have seen the basic components needed to connect multiple PCs to a network, it's time to try this in practise.

To prove your ability to create a PC network you need to be able to complete some specific tasks:

» Connect at least one PC to an existing network.

» Configure a PC to access a shared network drive.

» Configure a PC to access a shared printer.

The easiest way to demonstrate each task is to perform a walkthrough – a practical step-by-step guide which you will be able to follow.

## Connect at least one PC to an existing network

An existing network is two or more PCs connected together, either a peer-to-peer or client-server network. To keep things simple, let's assume we are connecting to a wired peer-to-peer network.

In order to connect to this, we will need:

» a workstation (with a wired network card)

» a Windows operating system (e.g., XP or Vista)

» a Category 5 Ethernet cable.

### Step 1
It is not normally necessary to switch off equipment to perform this action; however, if your school or college's health and safety guidelines recommend doing so, please do it before continuing.

Plug the Ethernet cable firmly into the workstation's network card socket.

### Step 2
Plug the other end of the Ethernet cable firmly into an empty socket in the switch (there may be many to choose from).

FIGURE 4.14 **Plugging Ethernet cable into Workstation's network card**

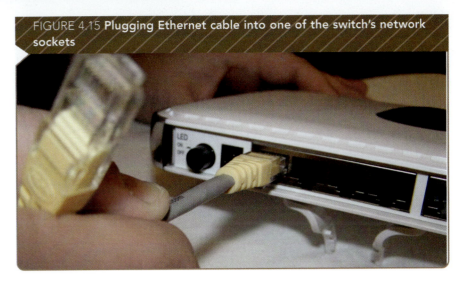

FIGURE 4.15 **Plugging Ethernet cable into one of the switch's network sockets**

You may notice small LEDs (light emitting diodes) on the switch or network card start to flash. This is normal, so don't worry!

### Step 3

At this point, your PC's operating system should detect an active network connection.

Each PC system connected to a network uses a unique IP (Internet protocol) network address. To ensure your PC is on the same network, it has to have an IP address in the same range as the other PCs connected to the switch.

An IP address takes the form of four groups of digits separated by full stops. These addresses vary from organisation to organisation but the first three groups of numbers are likely to be the same in any network.

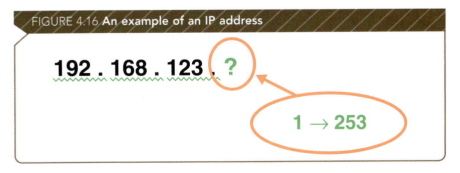

FIGURE 4.16 **An example of an IP address**

The following example shows how to set the PC's IP address in Windows Vista.

Click Start button and choose Control Panel.

On the Control Panel, chose Network and Sharing Centre.

FIGURE 4.17 Windows Vista – Control Panel

Click the 'Manage Network connections' link:

FIGURE 4.18 Windows Vista – Networking and Sharing Centre

The following dialogue box will ask you to select a network adapter. Usually just one wired network adapter will be shown.

FIGURE 4.19 Windows Vista – Network Connections

Right-click the network adapter and chose 'Properties' from the context menu that appears.

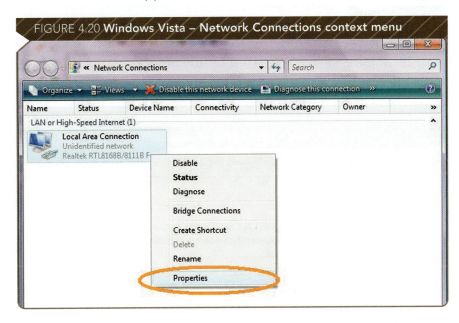

FIGURE 4.20 **Windows Vista – Network Connections context menu**

The next dialogue box that Windows Vista will display can look quite complex. Don't worry: we're only interested in one particular option. Select the 'Internet Protocol Version 4 (TCP/IPv4)' entry and click on the 'Properties' button.

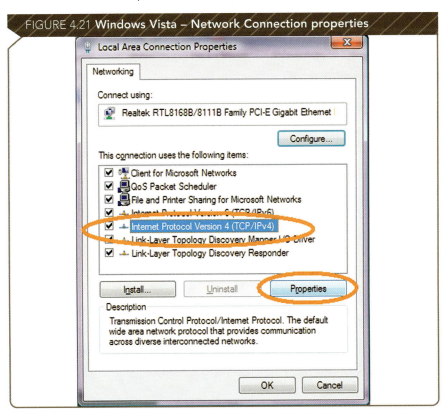

FIGURE 4.21 **Windows Vista – Network Connection properties**

The dialogue box that follows is where you need to key in the IP address.

As mentioned earlier, the first three groups of numbers must be the same on all PCs connected to the network; the last number must be unique – that is, not used by any other PC. If you don't know the IP address of the other PCs on the network, you can check these using the instructions given on pages 131–3.

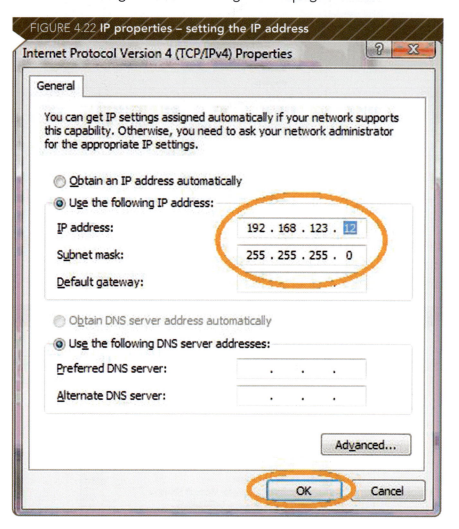

FIGURE 4.22 **IP properties – setting the IP address**

The Subnet mask should also be set to 255.255.255.0. If you click in the box, it is likely that Windows Vista will complete this for you automatically.

Click the 'OK' button to accept (finalise) these changes.

If you have completed these steps carefully, your PC should be successfully connected to an existing network.

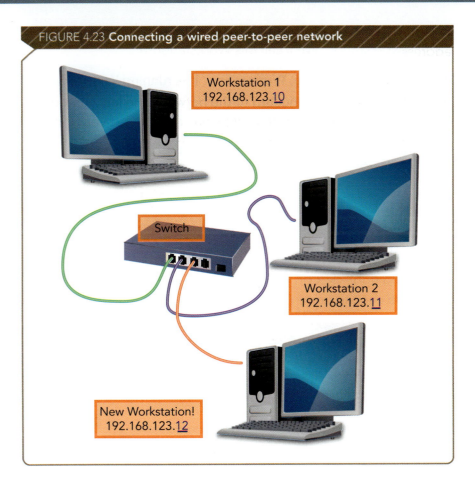

FIGURE 4.23 **Connecting a wired peer-to-peer network**

Workstation 1
192.168.123.10

Switch

Workstation 2
192.168.123.11

New Workstation!
192.168.123.12

Well done, you have successfully connected and configured a
wired peer-to-peer system!

**JOIN IN**

**Try to connect a PC workstation to an existing network.**

Start by gathering the appropriate components for a wired
network. Follow the step-by-step instructions above for
connecting these components and setting the correct network
addresses.

Were you successful?

**Write down any
problems you
experienced with this
activity and discuss
them with your
teacher/tutor.**

**LINKS**

## Configure a PC to access a shared
## network drive

A network drive is a common shared network resource, as are
printers. Although these resources are connected to one particular
workstation (or server), they can be shared with other users.

To connect to a network drive, it is necessary to share the drive on the first workstation. We'll call this Workstation '1'.

In the following example, Workstation '1' is running Windows XP and Workstation '2' is running Windows Vista. They are both connected in a wired peer-to-peer system.

Our goal is to share the G drive of Workstation '1' with Workstation '2'.

### Step 1

On Workstation '1', use 'My Computer' to see all the drives that are available.

You should right-click on the G drive. This will display a list of options to choose from.

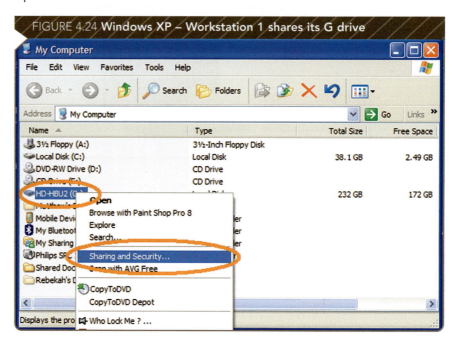

FIGURE 4.24 Windows XP – Workstation 1 shares its G drive

Select 'Sharing and Security…' from the list of options presented.

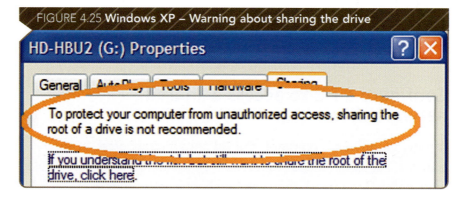

FIGURE 4.25 Windows XP – Warning about sharing the drive

### Step 2

Windows XP will display a warning about sharing the entire disk.
Click the link to continue.

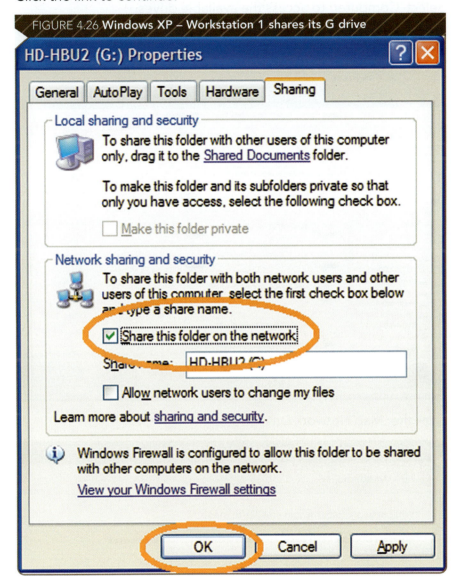

FIGURE 4.26 **Windows XP – Workstation 1 shares its G drive**

Click the 'Share this folder on the network' checkbox.

Then click the 'OK' button to finish.

### Step 3

The icon for the G drive will have changed in 'My Computer' to a
small open hand showing that the drive is shared.

You are now able to connect to the network drive from Workstation
'2'.

FIGURE 4.27
**Shared drive**

### Step 4

You can now use Workstation '2' to access the files on the G drive.

Select 'Computer' to access the available drives.

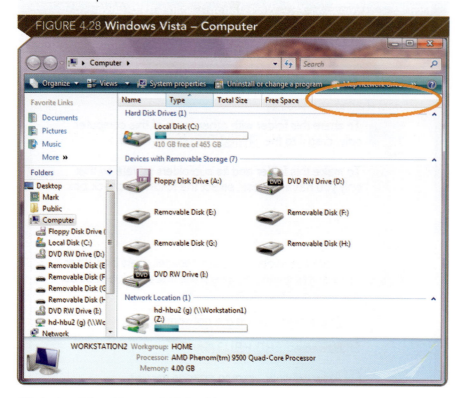

Click the 'Map Network Drive' button

Click the 'Browse' button.

### Step 5

You should see a list containing the workstations on the network (Workstations '1' and '2').

FIGURE 4.30 Windows Vista – Shared drives on Workstation 1

Clicking 'Workstation1' will show its shared network drive.

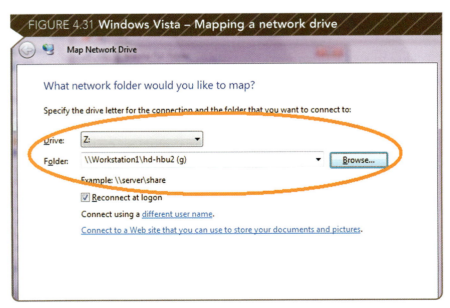

FIGURE 4.31 Windows Vista – Mapping a network drive

This would create a 'Z:' drive on Workstation '2' which is actually the shared network drive on Workstation '1'.

Click the 'Finish' button to complete the task.

### Step 6

It should now be possible to use Workstation '2' to access the files on Workstation '1'.

Select 'Computer' to access the available drives again.

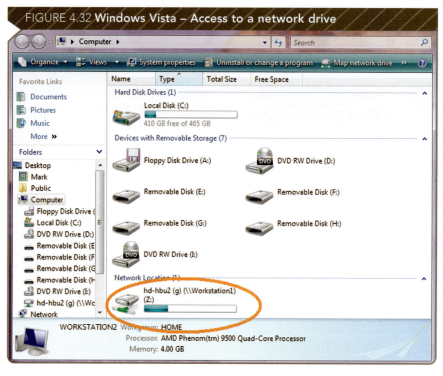

FIGURE 4.32 **Windows Vista – Access to a network drive**

This time you should be able to see a new Network Location.

Clicking this new drive icon '(Z:)' will access the network drive.

Try to share a workstation's drive on an existing network with another workstation.

Were you successful?

This can be carried out as a pair activity. In this instance, you should each complete and sign a witness statement that explains your partner's actions.

LINKS

# Configure a PC to access a shared printer

The following example demonstrates sharing a printer. It uses the same network as that used to share a network drive.

### Step 1

On Workstation '1', choose 'Printers and Faxes' to see all the printers that are available. Then right-click on the printer you want to share.

This will display a list of options to choose from.

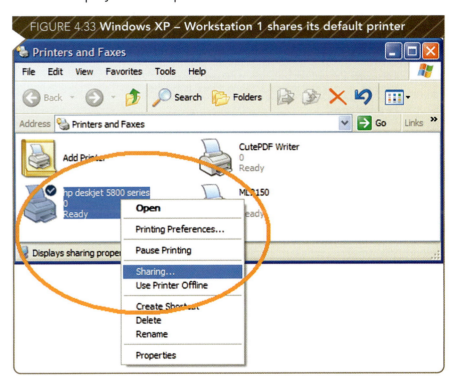

FIGURE 4.33 **Windows XP – Workstation 1 shares its default printer**

Select 'Sharing…' from the list of options presented.

### Step 2

The display will vary depending on the printer you wish to share.

You will first need to click the 'Share the printer' radio button and then key in a name for the printer share.

The example in Figure 4.34 uses 'hpdeskjet'.

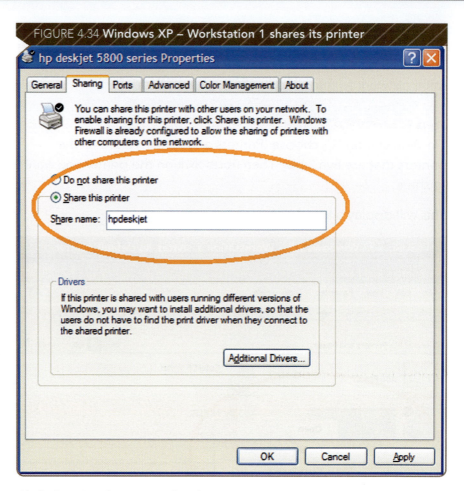

FIGURE 4.34 **Windows XP – Workstation 1 shares its printer**

Click the 'OK' button to finish.

### Step 3

The icon for the printer will have changed in 'Printers and Faxes' to a small open hand showing that the drive is shared.

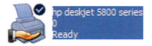

You are now able to connect to this printer from Workstation '2'.

### Step 4

You can now use Workstation '2' to access this printer.

Select 'Printers' in the 'Control Panel' to access the available drives.

*Step 5*

FIGURE 4.35 Windows Vista – Printers

Click on the 'Add a printer' button.

*Step 6*

Choose to a network printer.

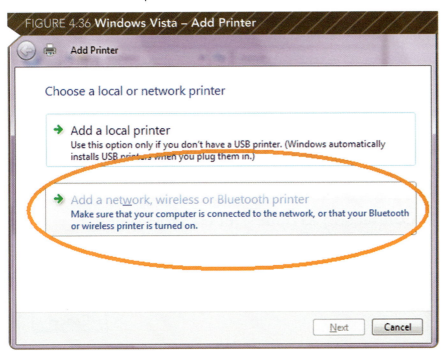

FIGURE 4.36 Windows Vista – Add Printer

Click 'Next' button to continue.

*Step 7*

Workstation '2' will scan the network for a shared printer. It will find the HP DeskJet shared by Workstation '1'.

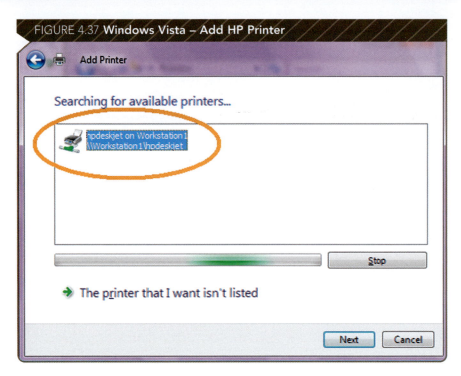

FIGURE 4.37 Windows Vista – Add HP Printer

Add Printer

Searching for available printers...

hpdeskjet on Workstation1
\\Workstation1\hpdeskjet

Stop

➔ The printer that I want isn't listed

Next     Cancel

Click on this printer's name.

Then click on the 'Next' button to continue.

### Step 8

Windows will then attempt to connect to the shared printer on Workstation '1'.

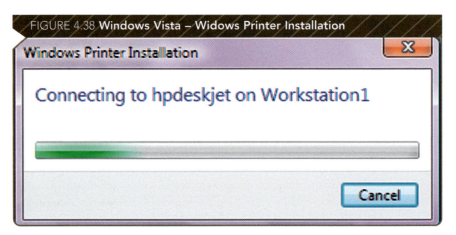

FIGURE 4.38 Windows Vista – Widows Printer Installation

Windows Printer Installation

Connecting to hpdeskjet on Workstation1

Cancel

Once this action has been completed, you should be able to print from Workstation '2' using the shared printer as long as both Workstation '1' and its printer are switched on.

**JOIN IN**

Try to share a workstation's printer on an existing network with another workstation.

Were you successful?

This can be carried out as a pair activity. In this instance you should each complete and sign a witness statement that explains your partner's actions.

**LINKS**

## Testing

Although connecting PC workstations to a network and sharing their resources is certainly a technical challenge, the most important thing to remember is that it doesn't always work properly - or as expected. Things often go wrong. It is, therefore, a good idea to test the functionality of the network and its shared resources.

The following are some simple tests to check for connection errors.

### Connectivity

Each workstation can be 'Pinged' to test connectivity.

Pinging works by sending a block of data from Workstation '1' to Workstation '2'. Workstation '2' will let Workstation '1' know if it has received the data successfully and how long the transfer took.

FIGURE 4.39 **Windows XP – Pinging another workstation**

```
C:\WINDOWS\system32\cmd.exe                           _ □ ✕

C:\>ping 192.168.123.11

Pinging 192.168.123.11 with 32 bytes of data:

Reply from 192.168.123.11 : bytes=32 time=9ms TTL=64
Reply from 192.168.123.11 : bytes=32 time=1ms TTL=64
Reply from 192.168.123.11 : bytes=32 time=2ms TTL=64
Reply from 192.168.123.11 : bytes=32 time=1ms TTL=64

Ping statistics for 192.168.123.11:
    Packets: Sent = 4, Received = 4, Lost = 0 (0% loss),
Approximate round trip times in milli-seconds:
    Minimum = 1ms, Maximum = 9ms, Average = 3ms
```

This tells us:

» if the physical connection is working properly (wired or wireless connection)

» if the network (IP) addresses are correctly configured

» how fast the connection is (by the time taken for Workstation '2' to say it has received the data).

It is unlikely that any other test will work if the simple ping test doesn't.

### Network drive access

Try to connect to the network drive and:

» copy a file from the network drive

» copy a file to the network drive.

The second option may not work if the shared drive hasn't had this permission correctly set.

### Network print access

The obvious test for a printer is to print documents (or a test page) from Workstation '2'.

Did it print correctly?

**MANAGE**

**Test the functionality of your two-workstation network by:**

✱ pinging each workstation using its network IP address

✱ copying files to and from a shared network drive

✱ printing a test page on a shared network printer.

Did your network perform as expected?

If not, what went wrong? Why do you think this happened?

## Simple problems

When working with networks, it is likely that you will encounter a number of different problems.

Typical problems include: a missing or out of data printer driver; connectivity problems and drives that are not mapped (or not mapped correctly).

Table 4.1 is an example of a simple form that could be used to record solutions to simple network problems.

TABLE 4.1 **Network Problems and Solutions record**

| Network Problems and Solutions | | |
|---|---|---|
| **Problem** | **Caused by** | **Try** |
| Shared printer not working | Printer not shared correctly. | Review share on workstation. |
| | Printer not added correctly to other workstation. | Add printer to workstation. |
| | Printer not using correct drivers. | Install the correct printer drivers. |
| Shared network drive not accessible | Drive isn't shared correctly. | Create a new drive share. |
| | Drive has not been mapped by other workstation. | Map a new network drive to the share. |
| Cannot see any other workstations on the network to share any resources | Does a ping test work correctly? | Review the network IP addresses on all workstations. |
| | Are all Ethernet cables correctly connected? | Ensure all cables are correctly inserted into workstations and switch. |
| | For Windows, are all workstations using the same workgroup name? | Add all workstations to the same workgroup. |

**TEAMWORK**

**Divide a group of friends or classmates into two teams.**

Team 1 builds a simple peer-to-peer network and then creates some deliberate problems for Team 2 to find. For example, they may partly disconnect an Ethernet cable or set wrong IP addresses.

Team 2 examines the network and tries to fix the problems, recording each 'repair' they make and the details of the problems they find.

**Write a formal record of this activity and place it in your portfolio. Remember to include the date.**

**LINKS**

## ...a help desk assistant

**Name:** Madelyn Watson

**Age:** 20 years

**Employer:** A large publishing company

**» What I do in my job as a help desk assistant:**

I take calls from workers who have problems with their workstation or connection to the company network. I try to solve their problems on the phone, but sometimes I have to visit them at their workstation. I record all calls on our database, along with details about the problem and any solutions to the problem that I've tried. I test the solution to make sure it works correctly

Sometimes I have to pass the problem to a more experienced colleague if none of the solutions I've tried work.

**» Qualifications:**

BTEC National Diploma for IT Practitioners
ECDL (European Computing Driving Licence)

**» What I like about my job:**

The subjects I liked most at school were IT and Maths. I'm really happy that I can use these skills to identify and fix problems with technical systems.

When people call the help line, they are often really unhappy. Their computer might have stopped working when they've got a rush job on. I need to be patient and understanding when dealing with these people. If I fix their problem, they're happy.

**» The hardest part of my job:**

This is when people get mad at me when I can't fix the problem. They think everything is easy to fix, even though they can't do it themselves! Sometimes I have to say I'll call them back because I need to get advice and then they keep calling me before I've been able to refer the problem to someone more experienced.

Also, I really don't like it when there are office moves and we have to take all the equipment from one floor, or office area, to another. We get lots of helpdesk calls after a move about silly little problems that the person could really have solved themselves.

Madelyn Watson

# Case Study

## BandStuff.com

The managers at BandStuff.com have asked you to look into networking their PCs.

They are not sure what equipment to buy or how to configure the PCs to share printers or folders.

To help them, complete the following tasks:

1. Design an A3 poster that shows the typical layout of a wired and wireless network.

2. Produce an A4, step-by-step booklet or a comic strip for setting up shares for printing and network drives.

3. Produce a wiki or electronic slideshow which explains the difference between peer-to-peer and client-server networks.

Present these documents to your teacher/tutor for feedback.

With this particular case study you will need to seek feedback from your teacher/tutor.

Once you have had this feedback, write up how you could have improved the documents and place all the evidence in your portfolio.

**F**or this unit you will need to present a portfolio that is a combination of coursework assignments, classwork and activities. Your teacher/tutor will award marks for the work you have submitted.

### Task One: Network components

You will have been given an assignment that asks you to produce a diagram showing the components needed to connect a PC to a network.

You should be able to identify each item and its function.

### Task Two: Connect to the network

Your practical assignment will concentrate on you demonstrating your ability to connect a PC to a network so that it can access shared network resources such as printers or scanners.

The connections need to be fully tested to make sure that the system works correctly.

Any problems you identified as part of the connection process should have been fully resolved.

# SUMMARY / SKILLS CHECK

**» Do you know how a PC is connected to a network?**

✔ In this technical unit you will have learned how to identify components of systems, specifically the components needed to link a PC to a network.

**» Are you able to connect a PC to an existing network and resolve simple problems?**

✔ As part of your practical activities you have connected at least one PC to an existing network.

✔ You have shown that you can configure a PC to access a shared network resource.

✔ It is important that you test installations carefully to make sure that they are fully operational and this unit has introduced you to three simple testing strategies:

– testing for connectivity

– testing network drive access

– testing network printer access.

✔ The final part of this unit has given you the opportunity to solve some simple networking problems such as out-of-date drivers, drive mapping or connectivity problems.

# OVERVIEW

Databases are an organisation's way of storing, and quickly retrieving, large amounts of information. They are an electronic form of filing cabinet and – just like using a filing cabinet – a database only works properly if you enter the information you want to store in a sensible way.

A database in computing uses special software to organise the storage of data (information). The information is organised in such a way that it is easy to manage, to access what you need and to update it when necessary. The sort of information a company might want to store in a database might include:

- » customers' records
- » financial records
- » a catalogue of products
- » a record of stock
- » images (for example, a picture library).

In this unit, you will find out how a basic single table database is structured. You will learn about data entry and how to maintain records through entering, editing and deleting information. You will also find out how to retrieve (take out) information in response to a query, to sort records and create and print simple reports.

# 05

# Database Systems

## Skills list

At the end of this unit, you should:

» be able to create a simple database system

» be able to use database tools to retrieve and present information

# Be able to create a simple database system

**A** database is a tool for storing information (data). Organisations need to store data such as customer's records, for example, or details about sales and stock. For data to be useful once it is stored, it has to be organised in a way that makes it easy to find again. Before electronic databases, data was often stored using paper files or cards that had to be created and edited manually.

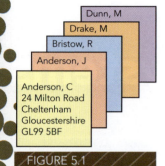

**FIGURE 5.1**
**Record cards**

### FIND OUT

What information do you think your school or college might store about you? See if you can find out.

Why do you think they need this information?

Talk to the adults in your family, or at your school or college. See if you can find another ten examples where information will be stored about you later in your life.

Data was usually stored alphabetically (A to Z) or numerically (1–100) so that, when needed, records could be found and retrieved easily. However, record cards could also be lost easily. Staff could take a card out of its position to make adjustments then replace it incorrectly. The card itself could be physically mislaid, or, on occasions, it could be damaged or destroyed. This meant that the next time the card was needed, it would not be available.

It was also difficult to create any sort of backup for the data as this would also have to be done manually. So, in the event of a disaster, such as a fire, many organisations faced losing all their organisational information.

## Why use a database?

Once a database has been organised (given a structure), data can easily be entered, updated and stored.

The data items can be manipulated so that they are presented in a way that will meet user needs. Users can sort the data alphabetically A to Z, then at the touch of a button can reverse the alphabet to display the data in reverse order Z to A. Data can be searched to find and retrieve (take out) specific records. Data can also be copied and pasted into other programs or into other databases.

It is easy to create datasbases. Large quantities of information about people can be stored electronically, taking up much less space than filing cabinets do.

## How is a single table database structured?

When data is stored in a database, it is organised into tables. Each table is made up of rows (records) and columns (fields).

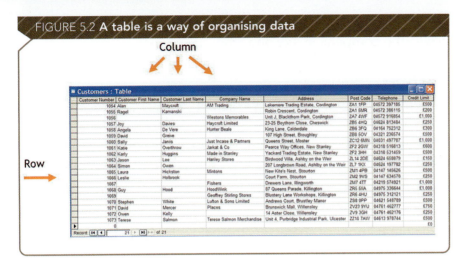

FIGURE 5.2 **A table is a way of organising data**

Each table has a focus. For example, Figure 5.2 is about customers. The table could also have been about suppliers or stock.

## Field

A field is a column in a database. Each field has a field heading; so that when the data is keyed in the same data items will be grouped together in the column; for example, all post codes can be held together in a single column.

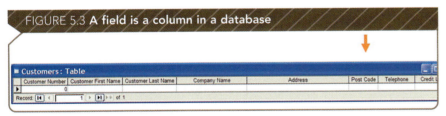

FIGURE 5.3 **A field is a column in a database**

As we will see later, the data is organised in this way so that it can be searched and sorted.

## Record

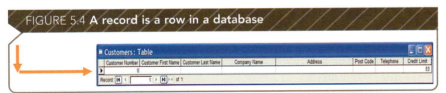

FIGURE 5.4 **A record is a row in a database**

In our example of a customer table, each row contains all the information we have about a single customer. This includes the customer's name, their company name (if they are not an individual customer), their address, post code, telephone number and their credit limit.

The credit limit is the maximum amount that a customer is allowed to owe the company at any one time.

## Data types

The type of data each field contains is set when the database is created. This is so that the data stored in the fields can be used in particular ways. For example, if a field is set as a number, it means that the user will be able to use the data in that field in calculations.

The text data type is unusual in that the user needs to specify the length of the field. This means that the user has to decide the maximum number of characters the field is likely to hold. As a general rule, count the number of characters (including any spaces) and add 2.

For example:

Bernie Fishpool would be 15 + 2, therefore 17 characters.

29 Dovetail Crescent, Manchester would be 32 + 2, therefore 34 characters.

Why add two? Because it is an easy number to remember and this will give you a little extra space if you have underestimated.

Once you have decided on the field names and data types you need for your database, you can create your table.

TABLE 5.1 **The main data types**

| Data type | Description |
|---|---|
| Currency | The user inputs a number, usually with decimal places, that represents a value in money. The relevant symbol that represents the type of currency is automatically added. For example, £ (pound), $ (dollar), € (euro). |
| Number | This field can be set with or without decimal places. With decimal places it is known as a real or floating point number. Without decimal places it is known as an integer. For example, 4.597 is a floating point number and 5 is an integer. |
| Date | There are variations, but it is usual to show the day (dd), month (mm) and year (yyyy). For example, 19/05/1992 would be a dd/mm/yyyy format. Note that Americans show the month before the day – mm/dd/yyyy. |
| Text | This field stores characters, symbols or numbers (as long as you do not need to calculate with them). |
| AutoNumber | This is the data type that automatically inserts sequential numbers into a field to provide a unique identifier. |
| Yes/No | This field stores values like true or false, yes or no, right or wrong. |

To create a table, open your database software (this will probably be Microsoft Access). Click on the 'Tables' option, and then on 'Create table in the Design view'.

Each field name can now be keyed in and the data type selected from a dropdown list. When working with a text field, remember to set the field size.

Once the fields have been set up, save the table.

## How is data entered?

Data can be entered directly into the table by viewing the table in datasheet view and moving between the columns and rows using the arrow or tab and enter keys.

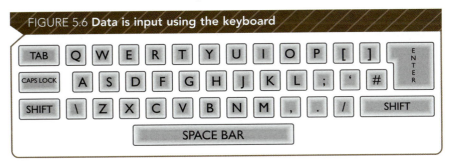

FIGURE 5.6 **Data is input using the keyboard**

To access the datasheet view of the table, simply double click it from the tables list.

FIGURE 5.5 **Database tables menu**

CHECK IT OUT

Find out what happens if you click on 'Table Design View'. What displays in 'Field Name' and 'Field Properties'?

FIGURE 5.7 **Datasheet view of the table**

**Customers : Table**

| Customer Number | Customer First Name | Customer Last Name | Company Name | Address | Post Code | Telephone | Credit Limit |
|---|---|---|---|---|---|---|---|
| 1054 | Alan | Maycroft | AM Trading | Lakemere Trading Estate, Cordington | ZA1 1FP | 04572 397185 | £500 |
| 1055 | Ragel | Kamanski | | Robin Crescent, Cordington | ZA1 5MR | 04572 386115 | £200 |
| 1056 | | | Westons Memorables | Unit J, Blackthorn Park, Cordington | ZA7 4WF | 04572 916854 | £1,000 |
| 1057 | Joy | Davies | Haycroft Limited | 23-25 Boythorn Close, Cheswick | ZB5 4HQ | 04624 813484 | £250 |
| 1058 | Angela | De Vere | Hunter Beale | King Lane, Calderdale | ZB6 3FQ | 04164 752312 | £300 |
| 1059 | David | Greive | | 107 High Street, Broughley | ZB8 5OV | 04321 236574 | £500 |
| 1060 | Sally | Jarvis | Just Incase & Partners | Queens Street, Moster | ZC12 6MN | 04031 497787 | £1,000 |
| 1061 | Katie | Overthrow | Jarkat & Co | Pearce Way Offices, New Stanley | ZF2 2GW | 04318 516813 | £600 |
| 1062 | Karly | Huggins | Made in Stanley | Yackard Trading Estate, New Stanley | ZF2 3HH | 04318 531459 | £500 |
| 1063 | Jason | Lee | Hanley Stores | Birdwood Villa, Ashby on the Weir | ZL14 2DE | 04624 658879 | £150 |
| 1064 | Simon | Owen | | 207 Longbrown Road, Ashby on the Weir | ZL7 1KX | 04624 197782 | £250 |
| 1065 | Laura | Hickston | Mintons | New Kite's Nest, Stourton | ZM1 4PB | 04147 145626 | £500 |
| 1066 | Leslie | Holbrook | | Court Farm, Stourton | ZM2 9VS | 04147 634578 | £250 |
| 1067 | | | Fishers | Drewers Lane, Illingworth | ZM7 4TT | 04219 574921 | £1,000 |
| 1068 | Guy | Hood | HoodWink | 87 Queens Parade, Killington | ZR5 5XA | 04975 336644 | £1,000 |
| 1069 | | | Geoffrey Stirling Stores | Blustery Lane Workshops, Killington | ZR6 4HU | 04975 312121 | £250 |
| 1070 | Stephen | White | Lufton & Sons Limited | Andrews Court, Brustley Manor | ZS8 0PP | 04621 548789 | £500 |
| 1071 | David | Mercer | Places | Brunswick Mall, Willensley | ZV23 9YU | 04761 462777 | £750 |
| 1072 | Owen | Kelly | | 14 Aster Close, Willensley | ZV9 3GH | 04761 462176 | £250 |
| 1073 | Terese | Salmon | Terese Salmon Merchandise | Unit 4, Purbridge Industrial Park, Ulcester | ZZ10 7AW | 04613 978744 | £500 |
| 0 | | | | | | | £0 |

Record: 21 of 21

### Data entry form

Because keying data directly into the table is not particularly user-friendly, most databases have a different view of the table called a 'form' to make data input easier.

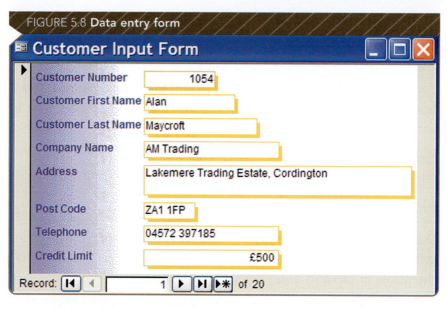

FIGURE 5.8 **Data entry form**

**Customer Input Form**

| | |
|---|---|
| Customer Number | 1054 |
| Customer First Name | Alan |
| Customer Last Name | Maycroft |
| Company Name | AM Trading |
| Address | Lakemere Trading Estate, Cordington |
| Post Code | ZA1 1FP |
| Telephone | 04572 397185 |
| Credit Limit | £500 |

Record: |◄ ◄ 1 ► ►| ►* of 20

When you use the input form, you find that you can only ever see **one** customer's details at a time. With the main table you can see many records at the same time. Using this interface makes inputting data much easier.

Regardless of whether the data is put directly into the table or into the database via the form, it will still be stored in the same place – the table view and the form view are just different ways of viewing the same data.

**REFLECT**

Think about where you use input forms when you use the computer. Think about the times you have found a form difficult or easy to use.

**Find five different examples of forms and print copies to put in your portfolio.**

LINKS

## Creating a simple database

We are now going to create a simple single table database for BandStuff.com. The table will hold information about the company's stock (see Figure 5.9).

### The table structure
First we must decide what information we want to hold about the stock. Let's look at the data that the organisation has provided.

FIGURE 5.9 **Bandstuff.com data**

| Description | Quantity | Price |
|---|---|---|
| T-shirts - Blue - L | 10 | £10.75 |
| T-shirts - Blue - M | 12 | £9.25 |
| T-shirts - Blue - S | 17 | £8.75 |
| T-shirts - Black - L | 8 | £10.75 |
| T-shirts - Black - M | 40 | £10.25 |
| T-shirts - Black - S | 26 | £9.75 |
| T-shirts - Red - L | 50 | £8.50 |
| T-shirts - Red - M | 50 | £8.00 |
| T-shirts - Red - S | 10 | £7.50 |
| T-shirts - Purple - L | 15 | £10.50 |
| T-shirts - Purple - M | 50 | £10.00 |
| T-shirts - Purple - S | 25 | £9.50 |
| Wristbands - Large | 10 | £5.00 |
| Wristbands - Medium | 34 | £4.50 |
| Wristbands - Small | 11 | £4.00 |
| Mugs - Blue | 1 | £3.50 |
| Mugs - Red | 17 | £3.50 |
| Mugs - Green | 9 | £3.50 |
| Mugs - Black | 12 | £3.50 |
| Mugs - Purple | 50 | £3.50 |

The company currently has twenty stock items and more will be added at a later date.

Figure 5.9 shows each stock item, how many the company currently holds in stock (quantity) and how much they sell them for (price).

The obvious data items to store are:

» Description

» Quantity

» Price.

These items will provide headings for the fields.

Looking at the data shown in Figure 5.9, you will notice that there is nothing in the table that can be used as a short reference code for the items, so we will add an extra field called StockID and give each item a number. It will be easier for staff using the database to refer to a stock item as item 4 than as 'T-shirts – Black – L'.

Therefore, when we create our database we will have four fields: StockID, Description, Quantity and Price.

## Choosing data types for the fields

Now that we know which fields we need to include, we must decide:

» what field names to use

» what data types or field formats (e.g. text, number, date) to use

» what field lengths (particularly in the case of text) to set.

**JOIN IN**

With a group of classmates, look at the stock data and agree what you think the data type choices should be (try not to look at the solution provided in table 5.2).

Organising this information into a table makes it is easier to read and most developers use this technique. The table is known as a data table.

TABLE 5.2 **Data table**

| Field name | Data type/ Field format | Field length | Additional information |
|---|---|---|---|
| StockID | AutoNumber | | A different number will be given to each stock item |
| Description | Text | 20 | This will be the description of each item |
| Quantity | Number (integer) | | How many we have in stock |
| Price | Currency (with 2 decimal places) | | How much each item costs |

## Creating the table for the Bandstuff.com database

» Open Microsoft Access.

» Click on 'File', then on 'New' and then on 'Blank Database'. You will automatically be required to enter a name as the 'File New Database' box comes up automatically. Enter a suitable name, and then click on 'Create'.

» Click on the 'Table' tab, and then finally on 'Create table in Design view'.

» Input each of the field names and set the properties (size, etc., as shown).

» When this is complete, save the table as 'Stock' and close.

## Using the database (record handling)

This section explains how to enter data, edit your database and test it.

### Input, or enter, data

» Open the table as a datasheet and input (key in) the records shown in the list provided by BandStuff.com (Figure 5.9).

» You will notice that as you finish keying each record and you press enter, the number of the next item will appear automatically.

» When you have finished keying in the records, close the table.

### Edit data

There are two main ways to edit a table – one is to add a record, the other is to change an existing record. We will look at each one here.

1. Add an additional record on the end of the list, as Bandstuff.com has a new stock item: Mugs – Yellow and Brown Stripe   90    3.50

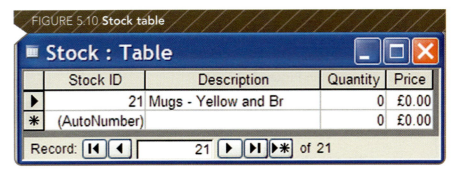

FIGURE 5.10 **Stock table**

You will notice that the system will truncate (shorten) the item description as there is insufficient space to display the whole item description.

Shorten the description to: Mugs – Yellow; and complete the record by entering the quantity (90) and price (£3.50).

2. The alternative is to increase the size of the text field.

Editing a record is relatively straightforward. Move to the record you wish to edit using the arrow keys. Highlight the item you want to edit, delete it and retype the new information. Or you can move the cursor into position and use the backspace and delete keys before typing in the text required.

We are going to edit record 18 which currently says 'Mugs – Orange'.

Use the cursor keys to the right position. Replace the colour Orange with the colour Yellow.

FIGURE 5.11 **Amended Stock table**

To complete the record-handling skills, you now need to delete a record.

Bandstuff.com has decided to stop selling red T-shirts. All current stock has been sold and the company want you to remove the records from the database. You need to delete records 7, 8 and 9.

To do this, highlight the records one by one, or all three at the same time.

Choose 'Edit' from the main menu then click on 'Delete'. The records will immediately disappear and a message box will appear as shown in Figure 5.12.

FIGURE 5.12 **Deletion confirmation box**

> **You are about to delete 3 record(s).**
>
> ⚠ If you click Yes, you won't be able to undo this Delete operation. Are you aure you want to delete these receords?
>
> [ Yes ]   [ No ]

The message asks you to confirm that this is what you want to do, and it reminds you that if you do this you will not be able to undo this action. If you are sure you have selected the right records, click on 'Yes'; otherwise click on 'No' and reselect.

Check that the records you wanted to delete have been deleted.

## Testing the database

Just as you would check your word-processed document for spelling and grammar, or the calculations in a spreadsheet to make sure that the spreadsheet is giving the right answers, you need to test your database.

A database should be tested in at least two ways:

» functionality

» fitness for purpose.

The test for functionality simply requires the developer to test and make sure that the database does what it is supposed to do and that everything works.

Testing for functionality includes testing that tables and forms open when buttons are pressed.

Some more complex databases might contain calculations. These must also be checked.

Later in this unit you will carry out search and sort activities. When testing for functionality, the results of these would also be checked to make sure that the search action gives the correct results and that the sort action puts the records in order correctly.

Deciding whether a database is fit for purpose requires the developer to answer two main questions:

» Is the database functioning as it should? (If not, it clearly would not be fit for purpose.)

» Is the user interface (what the user interacts with) easy to use?

Look at Figure 5.13. You could answer yes to the first question, but would have to say no to the second because the columns are not wide enough for the user to see all the detail. As the developer you would need to widen each column to make sure that all the data in the column was fully visible.

| Stock : Table | | | |
| Stock | Description | Quan | Price |
|---|---|---|---|
| 1 | T-shirts Blu | 10 | £9.75 |
| 2 | T-shirts Blu | 12 | £9.25 |
| 3 | T-shirts Blu | 17 | £8.75 |
| 4 | T-shirts Bla | 8 | £10.75 |
| 5 | T-shirts Bla | 40 | £10.25 |
| 6 | T-shirts Bla | 26 | £9.75 |
| 10 | T-shirts Pu | 15 | £10.50 |
| 11 | T-shirts Pu | 50 | £10.00 |
| 12 | T-shirts Pu | 25 | £9.50 |
| 13 | Wristbands | 10 | £5.00 |
| 14 | Wristbands | 34 | £4.50 |
| 15 | Wristbands | 11 | £4.00 |
| 16 | Mugs - Blu | 1 | £3.50 |
| 17 | Mugs - Rec | 17 | £3.50 |
| 18 | Mugs - Ora | 9 | £3.50 |
| 19 | Mugs - Bla | 12 | £3.50 |
| 20 | Mugs - Pur | 50 | £3.50 |
| 21 | Mugs - Yel | 50 | £3.50 |
| umber) | | 0 | £0.00 |

Record: 19

FIGURE 5.13 **User view of Stock table**

# Be able to use database tools to retrieve and present information

**A** database isn't much use unless you can work with the data and records that it stores. It would be like someone losing the key to a locked filing cabinet. You know that the information you want is probably inside the cabinet, but you have no way of getting at it.

The activities most often carried out on databases are searching (retrieving records based on a criterion) and sorting (ordering the records alphabetically or numerically).

Searching to extract records is done through a query.

## Query or Search

A query extracts records depending on the criterion (single data item) or criteria (multiple data items) that you are searching for.

To create a query, you click on the Create query in design view option, and then add the table you wish to query.

The fields to be displayed are chosen (notice we have not used them all) then the criteria are input.

In this case we are querying the database to display all records where the First Name is James.

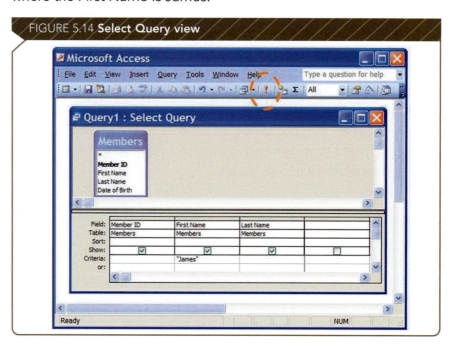

FIGURE 5.14 **Select Query view**

Once the query has been created, it needs to be run by clicking on the red exclamation mark icon on the menu bar.

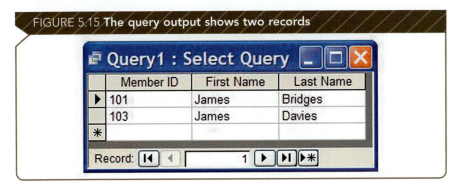

FIGURE 5.15 **The query output shows two records**

## Sort

The data can be sorted. You do this by clicking into one of the fields and then clicking on either the A to Z or Z to A icons.

FIGURE 5.16 **Sorting icons: A-Z and Z-A**

We can use our Stock table (see Figure 5.17 on page 166) to carry out a number of sort activities.

Sorting can be carried out by letter of the alphabet or by number, and in ascending or descending order.

An ascending sort puts the records in order from A to Z. As there is only one field that contains text in our example, we will do this sort on 'Description'.

Figure 5.18 shows the results of an ascending sort. You can see that the records have moved into a different order.

Using the same field, a descending sort orders the records from Z down to A.

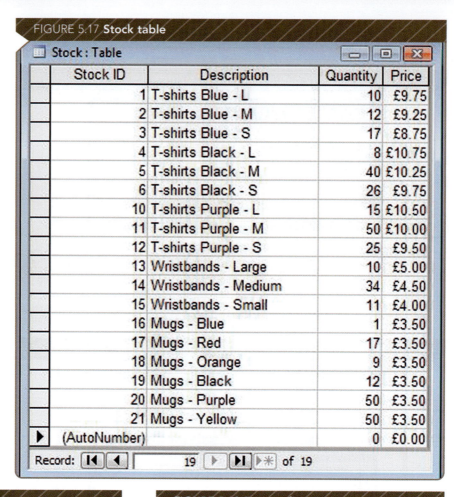

FIGURE 5.17 **Stock table**

**Stock : Table**

| | Stock ID | Description | Quantity | Price |
|---|---|---|---|---|
| | 1 | T-shirts Blue - L | 10 | £9.75 |
| | 2 | T-shirts Blue - M | 12 | £9.25 |
| | 3 | T-shirts Blue - S | 17 | £8.75 |
| | 4 | T-shirts Black - L | 8 | £10.75 |
| | 5 | T-shirts Black - M | 40 | £10.25 |
| | 6 | T-shirts Black - S | 26 | £9.75 |
| | 10 | T-shirts Purple - L | 15 | £10.50 |
| | 11 | T-shirts Purple - M | 50 | £10.00 |
| | 12 | T-shirts Purple - S | 25 | £9.50 |
| | 13 | Wristbands - Large | 10 | £5.00 |
| | 14 | Wristbands - Medium | 34 | £4.50 |
| | 15 | Wristbands - Small | 11 | £4.00 |
| | 16 | Mugs - Blue | 1 | £3.50 |
| | 17 | Mugs - Red | 17 | £3.50 |
| | 18 | Mugs - Orange | 9 | £3.50 |
| | 19 | Mugs - Black | 12 | £3.50 |
| | 20 | Mugs - Purple | 50 | £3.50 |
| | 21 | Mugs - Yellow | 50 | £3.50 |
| ▶ | (AutoNumber) | | 0 | £0.00 |

Record: ◄◄ ◄ 19 ► ►► ►* of 19

FIGURE 5.18 **Ascending sort**

**Stock : Table**

| | Stock ID | Description | Quantity | Price |
|---|---|---|---|---|
| ▶ | 19 | Mugs - Black | 12 | £3.50 |
| | 16 | Mugs - Blue | 1 | £3.50 |
| | 18 | Mugs - Orange | 9 | £3.50 |
| | 20 | Mugs - Purple | 50 | £3.50 |
| | 17 | Mugs - Red | 17 | £3.50 |
| | 21 | Mugs - Yellow | 50 | £3.50 |
| | 4 | T-shirts Black - L | 8 | £10.75 |
| | 5 | T-shirts Black - M | 40 | £10.25 |
| | 6 | T-shirts Black - S | 26 | £9.75 |
| | 1 | T-shirts Blue - L | 10 | £9.75 |
| | 2 | T-shirts Blue - M | 12 | £9.25 |
| | 3 | T-shirts Blue - S | 17 | £8.75 |
| | 10 | T-shirts Purple - L | 15 | £10.50 |
| | 11 | T-shirts Purple - M | 50 | £10.00 |
| | 12 | T-shirts Purple - S | 25 | £9.50 |
| | 13 | Wristbands - Large | 10 | £5.00 |
| | 14 | Wristbands - Medium | 34 | £4.50 |
| | 15 | Wristbands - Small | 11 | £4.00 |
| * | (AutoNumber) | | 0 | £0.00 |

Record: ◄◄ ◄ 1 ► ►► ►* of 18

FIGURE 5.19 **Descending sort**

**Stock : Table**

| | Stock ID | Description | Quantity | Price |
|---|---|---|---|---|
| ▶ | 15 | Wristbands - Small | 11 | £4.00 |
| | 14 | Wristbands - Medium | 34 | £4.50 |
| | 13 | Wristbands - Large | 10 | £5.00 |
| | 12 | T-shirts Purple - S | 25 | £9.50 |
| | 11 | T-shirts Purple - M | 50 | £10.00 |
| | 10 | T-shirts Purple - L | 15 | £10.50 |
| | 3 | T-shirts Blue - S | 17 | £8.75 |
| | 2 | T-shirts Blue - M | 12 | £9.25 |
| | 1 | T-shirts Blue - L | 10 | £9.75 |
| | 6 | T-shirts Black - S | 26 | £9.75 |
| | 5 | T-shirts Black - M | 40 | £10.25 |
| | 4 | T-shirts Black - L | 8 | £10.75 |
| | 21 | Mugs - Yellow | 50 | £3.50 |
| | 17 | Mugs - Red | 17 | £3.50 |
| | 20 | Mugs - Purple | 50 | £3.50 |
| | 18 | Mugs - Orange | 9 | £3.50 |
| | 16 | Mugs - Blue | 1 | £3.50 |
| | 19 | Mugs - Black | 12 | £3.50 |
| * | (AutoNumber) | | 0 | £0.00 |

Record: ◄◄ ◄ 1 ► ►► ►* of 18

Figure 5.19 shows the results of a descending order sort. You will notice that that data has been turned upside down and is the exact reverse of the list shown in Figure 5.18.

We have a few more choices about the fields we can use for a numerical sort. For example, we can carry out an ascending numerical sort on 'Price'.

Figure 5.20 shows the items in the order of the cheapest first and the most expensive item last.

Our final sort will be a descending numerical sort on 'Quantity'. This sort shows us which stock items we have most of and which we have fewest of.

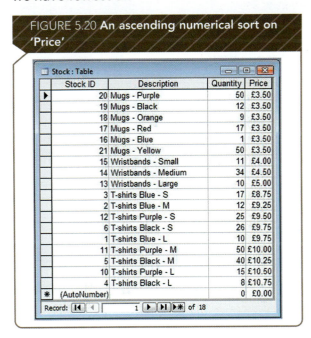

FIGURE 5.20 **An ascending numerical sort on 'Price'**

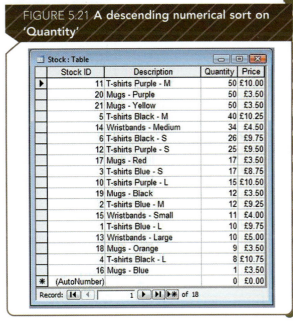

FIGURE 5.21 **A descending numerical sort on 'Quantity'**

## How do we present data from a database?

There are two main ways to output information from a database – viewing them in their datasheet, or as a report.

### Datasheet view

To view data in the datasheet view (Figure 5.22), we simply open the Query or the Table (Figure 5.23).

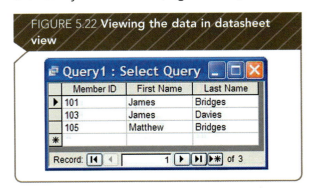

FIGURE 5.22 **Viewing the data in datasheet view**

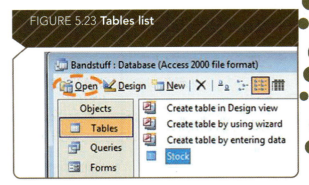

FIGURE 5.23 **Tables list**

### Report

The alternative way of viewing tables or queries is to view the output as a report, with headings. You might, for example, choose to sort customers in ascending order based on their Post Code. All the postcodes in our post code field begin with Z. Therefore, the program will sort on the second letter – beginning with ZA and ending with ZZ.

FIGURE 5.24 **A section taken from a customer data ordered by Post Code Report**

## Customer Data ordered by Post Code

| Customer Number | Customer First Name | Customer Last Name | Company Name | Address | Post Code | Telephone | Credit Limit |
|---|---|---|---|---|---|---|---|
| 1054 | Alan | Maycroft | AM Trading | Lakemere Trading Estate, Cordington | ZA1 1FP | 04572 397185 | £500 |
| 1055 | Ragel | Kamanski | | Robin Crescent, Cordington | ZA1 5MR | 04572 386115 | £200 |
| 1056 | | | Westons Memorables | Unit J, Blackthorn Park, Cordington | ZA7 4WF | 04572 916854 | £1,000 |
| 1057 | Joy | Davies | Haycroft Limited | 23-25 Boythorn Close, Cheswick | ZB5 4HQ | 04624 813484 | £250 |
| 1058 | Angela | De Vere | Hunter Beale | King Lane, Calderdale | ZB6 3FQ | 04164 752312 | £300 |
| 1059 | David | Greive | | 107 High Street, Broughley | ZB8 5OV | 04321 236574 | £500 |
| 1060 | Sally | Jarvis | Just Incase & Partners | Queens Street, Moster | ZC12 6MN | 04031 497787 | £1,000 |
| 1061 | Katie | Overthrow | Jarkat & Co | Pearce Way Offices, New Stanley | ZF2 2GW | 04318 516813 | £600 |
| 1062 | Karly | Huggins | Made in Stanley | Yackard Trading Estate, New Stanley | ZF2 3HH | 04318 531459 | £500 |
| 1063 | Jason | Lee | Hanley Stores | Birdwood Villa, Ashby on the Weir | ZL14 2DE | 04624 658879 | £150 |
| 1064 | Simon | Owen | | 207 Longbrown Road, Ashby on the Weir | ZL7 1KX | 04624 197782 | £250 |
| 1065 | Laura | Hickston | Mintons | New Kite's Nest, Stourton | ZM1 4PB | 04147 145626 | £500 |
| 1066 | Leslie | Holbrook | | Court Farm, Stourton | ZM2 9VS | 04147 634578 | £250 |
| 1067 | | | Fishers | Drewers Lane, Illingworth | ZM7 4TT | 04219 574921 | £1,000 |
| 1068 | Guy | Hood | HoodWink | 87 Queens Parade, Killington | ZR5 5XA | 04975 336644 | £1,000 |
| 1069 | | | Geoffrey Stirling Stores | Blustery Lane Workshops, Killington | ZR6 4HU | 04975 312121 | £250 |

Page 1 of 2

| Customer Number | Customer First Name | Customer Last Name | Company Name | Address | Post Code | Telephone | Credit Limit |
|---|---|---|---|---|---|---|---|
| 1070 | Stephen | White | Lufton & Sons Limited | Andrews Court, Brustley Manor | ZS8 0PP | 04621 548789 | £500 |

The report shown in Figure 5.24 is a two-page report. The user was asked to input a report heading as part of the report creation process. The page numbers are input automatically.

In your work setting, ask to see your employer's database. Talk to anyone who uses the database regularly.

» What does the company store information about?

» What do the users do with the data (create reports, query the data)?

# I want to be...

# ...a database developer

**Name:** Kim Shah

**Age:** 24 years

**Employer:** Freelance database developer

**»** **Qualifications:**

1 A level
BTEC National Diploma for IT Practitioners
A degree in Business Computer Systems

**»** **What do you do as a database developer?**

I investigate any specific user needs so that I can design a database that exactly meets those needs. I create both the database and the user interface so that people are able to get information when they need it, edit it or add to it.

At the end of it all, I test the database to make sure it works properly and that there are no glitches in the system.

I run regular checks to make sure that data is secure. I also maintain and update the database as needed and give support to anyone having problems using it.

**»** **Why did you become a database developer and what do you bring to your job?**

I love organising things – my friends call me the spreadsheet queen! Towards the end of secondary school, I knew I wanted to work in something to do with IT. When I found out about databases, and the jobs available in developing them, I just knew that's what I wanted to do.

I'm a good communicator, and really good at working out what people need from an IT system like a database. Although most of my work in developing the database is done on my own, I'm also good at working as part of a team – a skill that I need when trying to find out what users need from the database and how they will interact with it.

Time management is also an important skill for this job. There can be a lot of pressure to deliver products in a short time and you really don't want to compromise on the quality because of lack of time.

Kim Shah

# Case Study

BandStuff.com →

The managers at BandStuff.com have asked you to help them develop another part of their system by organising a simple table in a database where they will be able to store information about their suppliers.

Suppliers are the companies that BandStuff.com buys stock from. This includes T-shirts, mugs and wristbands, and will shortly also include the new range of hoodies.

You've been given two sample documents that BandStuff.com currently uses to store information about suppliers. These are:

» a record card – a card is created each time a new supplier is taken on

» a credit limit sheet – a single sheet of paper that lists all suppliers and the credit limit that BandStuff.com has with each company.

Look carefully at this data and then decide how you will organise your database.

Completing this case study activity will improve your database skills and also provides you with evidence for your portfolio.

FIGURE 5.25 **ABC Record card and Credit limit sheet**

Supplier Name: ABC Supplies

Address: Waterman Building, Horsham Road, Willesden, Nottingham

Post Code: WL8 2HP

Telephone Number: 04754 526454 Ext 673

Main Contact: Emma

**CREDIT LIMIT SHEET**

| Supplier Name | Credit Limit |
|---|---|
| ABC Supplies | £2,500 |
| Broadway & Co | £1,000 |
| Clifton Trading | £3,000 |
| Danby Icons | £500 |
| Jones Transfers | £1,500 |
| Limos Limited | £2,000 |
| Pride Pottery | £3,000 |
| Quinlan Shirts | £2,500 |
| Roberts & Son | £2,750 |
| Vic Transfers | £1,225 |
| ZZB Partners | £1,500 |

TABLE 5.3 **Case Study Data Table**

| Field name | Data type/Field format | Field length |
|---|---|---|
| Supplier ID | AutoNumber | |
| Supplier name | Text | 20 |
| Address | Text | 40 |
| Post code | Text | 10 |
| Telephone number | Text | 15 |
| Main contact | Text | 20 |
| Credit limit | Currency (No decimal places) | |

N.B. This is only one possible solution. Your data table might look different as you may well have decided on different field lengths.

# Case Study

| TABLE 5.4 Data for the Case Study | | | | | |
|---|---|---|---|---|---|
| Supplier name | Address | Post code | Telephone number | Main contact | Credit limit |
| ABC Supplies | Waterman Building Horsham Road Willesden Nottingham | WL8 2HP | 04754 526454 Ext 673 | Emma | £2,500 |
| Broadway & Co | Milton House Marlbury Swindon | ML23 9SA | 05132 516154 | John or James | £1,000 |
| Clifton Trading | Kelly Industrial Estate Rowberry Road Clifton | CL29 0NX | 06124 212452 | Rhani | £3,000 |
| Danby Icons | India Road Holton | HL59 2NQ | 04892 521759 | Hubert | £500 |
| Jones Transfers | High Street Fulton Killington | KL17 8MB | 04621 515631 | Millie | £1,500 |
| Limos Limited | Johnsborough Road Marlbury Swindon | ML24 6QW | 05132 321784 | Sonia | £2,000 |
| Pride Pottery | Tinsham Kiln Stourton Killington | KL21 4FF | 03147 618712 | Mark | £3,000 |
| Quinlan Shirts | Fanham Street Overton | OV61 7XC | 04547 523151 | Emmie | £2,500 |
| Roberts & Son | Naunton Business Park Marlbury Swindon | ML23 2FQ | 05132 363779 | Harry | £2,750 |
| Vic Transfers | Ravenscroft Meadow Lane Bridgenorton | BR44 0MV | 05467 518924 | Ebba | £1,225 |
| ZZB Partners | Sandy Road Beachburn Hinton | HN19 8UY | 05472 697333 | Aimee | £1,500 |

# Questions

1. Identify:

 – what field names you will use

 – what data types or field formats (for example, text, number, date) to use

 – what field lengths (particularly in the case of text) to set.

2. Create a data table (Figure 5.2 is given as an example).

3. Create a new database.

4. Create a database table using your data table as a guide.

5. Key in the data provided in Table 5.3.

6. Create a report of all suppliers in descending (highest to lowest) order of credit limit (remember to give the report a suitable heading). To do this, select the 'Reports' option from the main menu. Click on 'Create Report by using Wizard'. Carefully follow the instructions, taking special care to select the right options.

7. Create a query that lists only those suppliers based in Marlbury (your query view should show three records). To do this, select the 'Query' option from the main menu. Click on 'Create Query by using Wizard'. Carefully follow the instructions taking special care to select the right options.

8. Save and close your database.

9. Print the results of your query and report and show them to your teacher/tutor. Discuss anything you might improve if you do this exercise again.

# ✓ Assessment Tips

For this unit, you will be assessed by your teachers/tutors. It will definitely help if you have completed the Case Study activity.

### Task One: Create and use a database

» You will be given an assignment that asks you to create a simple database system to be used in a business situation.

» You will decide the field names, data types and field lengths for each of the table's columns and you may be asked to put your choices into a database table, as shown in this unit.

» You will be asked to create the structure of the database table.

» Data will be provided for you to enter into your database.

» Once the data has been entered you will be asked to edit one or more records, and delete a record.

### Task Two: Retrieve and present information

» Using the same database, you will be asked to make use of database tools.

» You will search and retrieve records using a query.

» You will use sorting techniques to present the same information in different ways.

» You must make sure that the data is presented in an acceptable way.

# SUMMARY / SKILLS CHECK

**» Creating a simple database system**

✓ Creating databases requires considerable skills. You will need to understand the data that the database will store. You will also decide how best to organise it to make sure that the data can be retrieved and used in whatever way the organisation needs.

✓ These skills can be learned as a set of rules and techniques that you can apply to almost any set of data.

✓ This unit has shown you how to set up and create a structure for a database. It has also shown you how to create a user-friendly interface by allowing users to enter data through a data entry form. Using this technique ensures that even new users can make good use of the database.

✓ The most important aspects of data handling are entering, editing and deleting records. However, care should always be taken when deleting records to ensure that the correct records are removed from the system.

**» Using database tools to manipulate data**

✓ Advanced data manipulation is achieved through searching and sorting the data stored in the database, and presenting the information in a useful way.

✓ The tools, techniques and skills you have learned from this unit can be transferred to a variety of applications. For example, the functions of search and sort are also available in word processing and spreadsheets.

# OVERVIEW

We see or use multimedia products every day. We might use the Internet, watch TV or play a computer game. Or we might pass a multimedia advert on the side of a bus shelter or get a Flash animation advert sent to our mobile phone.

This unit will help you become 'multimedia aware'. It will help you to recognise where multimedia is used and to identify the features that make it effective. You will learn about:

» how multimedia is used in business

» how to design and develop multimedia products

» how to test multimedia products

» how to seek feedback from test users to identify where products can be improved.

Your teacher/tutor will give you coursework assignments to do. You might also be given activities, or you can do some of the activities included in this book.

Your evidence will build into a portfolio that you will need to plan and organise. You should set yourself realistic goals for the development of your portfolio and you will need to discuss your own performance and progress with your teacher/tutor at regular intervals.

# 06

# Multimedia

# Know how multimedia is used in business

## What is multimedia?

Multimedia is the term used to describe devices that have an output that is a combination of any or all of the following:

» sound

» animation

» still images (like photographs)

» moving images (like film clips).

Some multimedia devices also have functionality that allows the user to manipulate text and data, and in some cases to add voice or speech.

**THINK**

Make a list of the multimedia devices you have in your home.

**L I N K S**

Use the list to make a table and write a brief explanation of the main features of each device. Put this in your portfolio.

## What are the business uses for multimedia?

### *Promotion and advertising*

There are many different ways of using multimedia to advertise and promote products and services. Here are some simple examples.

Digital photographs are now so easy to produce that most advertisements for products carry a picture. Which of the adverts on page 179 is more likely to result in a sale?

Both advertisements contain the same text. The only difference is one is more eye-catching because of the inclusion of the image. Sometimes advertisements will be created using library images (images that belong to the company) rather than a picture of the actual product.

Another way of using digital media in advertising might be to

FIGURE 6.1 **Advert with image**

FOR SALE - Renault Megane
Cabriolet Coupé 2005
Low mileage.  Recently serviced. Central locking.
Alloys.  One owner from new.
Contact: 05555 555555

FIGURE 6.2 **Advert without image**

FOR SALE - Renault Megane
Cabriolet Coupé 2005
Low mileage.  Recently serviced. Central locking.
Alloys.  One owner from new.
Contact: 05555 555555

create a video advert using a digital camera. The advertisement
could be for a product that you have invented or it could be for an
existing product. Or you might like to create an advertising video
for your school or town. In this instance you will make significant
use of editing software.

## Sales/promotion of a product

FIGURE 6.3 **Original poster**

FIGURE 6.4 **Final poster**

Most of the digital media that we have already explored can be used in the preparation or distribution of sales information. This could be as a flyer or full-sized poster.

The above sample poster began with a photograph of a man wearing a hoodie. The photograph, taken and stored digitally, was then manipulated to produce the final image and poster.

The flyer or poster might be distributed by attaching an electronic version to an email, printing it out from a file or using it on a page on the Internet.

### Web pages

Web pages also fall into the category of multimedia. This is particularly true of websites like www.youtube.com. YouTube is a multimedia website where users can upload their own video material and view material uploaded by others.

**With a group of classmates or friends, find five good examples of multimedia websites.**

Each of these sites should be a combination of at least three of the possible features, for example sound, moving image and text.

**Create a table of this information and keep a copy in your portfolio.**

L I N K S

### Virtual tours

Estate agents and travel companies can make videos of the inside of houses and flats and can take customers on virtual tours of properties. This can be done through the creation of DVDs, using a digital video camera like the one shown in Figure 6.5.

FIGURE 6.5 **Digital video camera**

ASK

**The following websites provide virtual tours of these famous places. Visit each one!**

Number 10 Downing Street
www.number-10.gov.uk/ – navigate to the interactive map

Disneyland Paris
www.disneylandparis.co.uk/ – scroll down to 'Your No10 tour'

The Great Wall of China
www.thebeijingguide.com/great_wall_of_china/

**With a group of classmates, create a five-minute virtual tour of your school or college.**

**Present this to your teacher/tutor and to the rest of your class.**

L I N K S

Like virtual tours, simple digital photographs can take you to places you might never otherwise have an opportunity to see.

This digital image is of the Dénia Castle in Spain which was built in the 11th century.

FIGURE 6.6 **Dénia Castle**

EarthCam has enabled us to look at other parts of the world from the comfort of our own homes. The cameras in Times Square, New York, for example, consist of multiple fixed and robotic systems offering a series of views that are updated every few seconds, with other cameras providing live streaming video and live sound from the city.

FIGURE 6.7 **Times Square Cam**

**JOIN IN**

Think about a place you would really like to visit.

Find a website that offers you a virtual tour of this holiday destination or building.

Take the tour!

With a group of friends or classmates, identify one advantage and one disadvantage of using this technology. Ask your group members to explain their views.

**L I N K S**

# What are some educational uses for multimedia?

### Games and e-learning packages

The Internet, in particular, has created a massive increase in the amount of digital educational material that has become accessible for parents, teachers/tutors and learners. This material includes both fun and serious games that have an educational theme.

The example shown in Figure 6.8 is of an interactive storybook that helps teach younger children to read.

FIGURE 6.8 **Interactive reading website**

There are three sentences on each page. The child can either read each one, or click on the sentence or speaker icon and hear it read out loud. The third sentence in each sequence contains a blank. Other words can then be dragged and dropped into the blank and the sentence will be read three ways – once with each word.

This particular website also contains a range of activities to support other school subjects such as Maths and Science.

### Interactive whiteboards

Another multimedia device now frequently used in schools and colleges is the interactive whiteboard.

FIGURE 6.9 **Interactive whiteboard**

The board has an image projected onto it, and the interactive technology allows the teacher/tutor to turn pages, write on the image, highlight aspects of the image, etc. These are now replacing the traditional whiteboards.

A real benefit of this technology is that the projected image can come from almost anywhere. It can come from work the teacher/tutor has prepared, or from the Internet, or from an e-book or podcast. It can also come directly from the learners' own work.

### Simulations

Using multimedia technology allows teachers/tutors to simulate experiences. For example, using webcams and microphones you could simulate a job interview or interviewing a client about IT needs.

## How is multimedia used in entertainment and leisure?

The leisure industry, in particular, has been revolutionised through the development of multimedia.

Users can play games online, download music or video clips, or access social websites to chat with friends.

Using head-mounted displays, motion trackers and data gloves, a player can physically become part of a computer game!

**CAUTION!**
If you do not know the person you are talking to over the Internet you should NEVER let the other person see you.

**ASK**

**What are:**

* head mounted displays?

* motion trackers?

* data gloves?

Write up your research and put it in your portfolio. Remember to include your sources of information.

L I N K S

## Be able to design, develop and test simple multimedia products

### What is a multimedia product?

It might be a digital video of a virtual tour of a sports centre, or a website containing digital photos of your school or local town.

It could be a presentation about your course for other learners containing a sound file of you or your classmates describing the course. It could be an advertisement for a school dance or for a sports event.

To show that you can design, develop and test a range of multimedia products you will need to create one of the following with limited interactivity.

» digital poster

» short animation

» advertisement

» quiz

» presentation

» simple movie.

What does limited interactivity mean? It means that there is no real requirement for users to interact with the product you create.

Before you begin to design your product, it would be useful to write down what you think the product is going to be and who it will be for (the target audience).

FIGURE 6.10 **Multimedia product idea form**

| Product title: | |
|---|---|
| **Product description:** | |
| **Purpose of product:** | |
| **Target audience (e.g., parents, customers, the public):** | |
| **Digital media to be used:** | |

Using a form like the one shown in Figure 6.10 might help you to decide on what you are going to do.

### How do you use the form?
Firstly, give your product a name.

Then write out what it is (a description).

Explain what it does (its purpose).

Describe who will use this product (its target audience).

Give a brief overview of the digital media you will use to create the product, e.g. camera, DVD camera, microphone, a particular type of software. A completed form might look like Figure 6.11

FIGURE 6.11 **A completed form**

| Product title: | School/college presentation for new students |
| --- | --- |
| **Product description:**<br>A 12-slide presentation about the school or college. The product should be stand alone (not require any user intervention). This can be achieved through timing the movement between slides, and creating a carousel to return the presentation to the beginning when the last slide has been shown. | |
| **Purpose of product:** | To inform new students about the school and what it has to offer. |
| **Target audience (e.g., parents, customers, the public):** | New students and parents. |
| **Digital media to be used:** | Microsoft PowerPoint, short video of the school grounds, photographs, a short speech by a current student, editing software. |

Once you have finalised your idea, you need to work through the process of developing the product. This process usually begins with a design.

# The development process

### Design
It will really help you create your product if you begin by designing what it will be like.

You can do this by writing a simple description, such as a series of steps that will need to be completed.

You could create diagrams such as flow charts that explain the different steps. You could also create a storyboard which is a visual design tool.

### What is a storyboard?

A storyboard is a series of images that represent what the product will look like, sometimes combined with arrows that show how the product will move between screens. This technique is frequently used in computer programming, website and computer games design.

FIGURE 6.12 **A storyboard**

The storyboard in the example was finally used to create an animation about twins. Neither one knows that the other exists until one day a sequence of events leads to them meeting. The items outlined in red (mostly arrows) also show the directional movement where it occurs.

The storyboard can be created using software or can be hand drawn. The important thing is that it provides a series of visual images that map out the content and the layout of the final product.

It is likely that, when creating your own product, you will use a number of different techniques to record your decisions.

### How will you develop your product?

You need to create the actual product using appropriate multimedia devices and software tools. As you may choose to create any sort of product, we will demonstrate how to use some of the media software that you may need to use to modify your images, movies or sound files.

### Create the product using appropriate software tools

The type of software you will use to create the basic product will depend on what that product is.

Capturing the media will be done via a digital camera for photographs, a digital video camera for video clips, and a microphone for sound files. The software that actually does these tasks will vary depending on the equipment you use. These days the equipment is mostly automatic and you will probably only need to point and press.

### Edit (working with graphics)

Once you have taken your photograph, you open it as an image in the software, in this case Adobe Photoshop Elements 6.

The first problem we have with our image is that it is too dark. The picture is actually of Edinburgh Castle, but it is underexposed (not enough light was available). To begin with, we choose Adjust Lighting, an option on the Enhance menu. We can then choose Brightness/Contrast to adjust the image. On the right of the window, there are a number of other effects we could apply.

FIGURE 6.13 **Photoshop**

Figure 6.14 and Table 6.1 explain what tools are available in Photoshop.

FIGURE 6.14 **Photoshop tools**

TABLE 6.1 **This is what each icon on the toolbar does**

| Tool | Description |
|---|---|
| **Navigation and measuring tools** | |
| Zoom | Makes the image bigger or smaller as required, allowing you to see more or less detail |
| Hand | Clicking and holding down the left mouse button allows you to move the image in the window |
| Eyedropper | This lets you copy or sample a colour from an image – the colour appears in the set foreground colour window – the process only copies the colour and not any texture information |
| **Selection tools** | |
| Rectangular marquee | This tool allows you to select only a portion of the image so that, when you then apply any of the retouching or painting options, only those parts of the image inside the marquee will be affected |
| Magnetic lasso | Allows you to lasso an object by drawing a line around it – you can then copy and paste it somewhere else without the rest of the image, or you can edit just what is inside or outside the lasso |
| Magic wand | The magic wand creates a line around the object for you just by clicking the icon and applying to the image – it chooses where the line will be |
| Quick selection | Quick selection is almost a combined option of lasso and wand in that it chooses an outline automatically but it then allows you to change the edges to capture only the bits you want |
| **Type tools** | |
| Horizontal type | Places text on the image |
| **Crop tools** | |
| Crop | This tool allows you to cut away the unwanted edges of an image |
| Cookie cutter | Like a cookie cutter used in baking, the cutter will cut out a part of the image in a chosen shape |
| Straighten | Clicking this tool will automatically straighten the image – you will probably need to crop it afterwards |
| **Retouching tools** | |
| Red eye removal | Removes the bright glowing red eye problem often experienced with flash photography |
| Spot healing brush | This tool lets you heal an image by automatically sampling colour and texture on either side of the problem area and blending the colours and textures to make the blemish disappear – for example, you could use this technique to remove creases in fabric, or pen lines on an image |
| Clone stamp | The clone stamp tool copies an area of the image including colour and texture and allows you to paste it elsewhere in the image |
| Eraser | Clicking the left mouse button and dragging the eraser across any area of the object will remove the colour |
| Blur and sponge | The blur and sponge tools are used to soften parts of the image |
| **Painting and drawing tools** | |
| Brush | The brush tool allows you to draw on your image – the colour is selected from the foreground colour options palette |
| Paint bucket | Fills a drawn shape or highlighted area with the colour chosen in the foreground colour option |
| Gradient | This tool is used to show the colour range as one colour changes into another or as a single colour graduates from dark to light |
| **Colour tools** | |
| Set foreground colour | Clicking on this icon allows you to access the colour palette and select up to two colours – each colour is put into one of the squares and clicking on the tiny arrows to the top right of this icon allows you to toggle (move) between the colours |
| **Shape tools** | |
| Custom shape | Outlines an area on your image in that particular shape |

If you look carefully at Figure 6.14, you will notice that some of the icons have a small black triangle to the bottom right. If you right click on any of the icons that contain a triangle you will find further options similar to the one on the main icon.

The best way to learn what these different tools do and the effects that they allow you to use is to experiment with the software and a few images. Using different tools allows you to adjust the picture. The original picture of Edinburgh Castle has been edited and the adjusted image shows the castle much more clearly.

FIGURE 6.15 **Edinburgh Castle (unedited)**

FIGURE 6.16 **Edinburgh Castle (edited)**

**TRY THIS**

Work on a copy of the image, not on the original, in case you make mistakes you cannot undo!

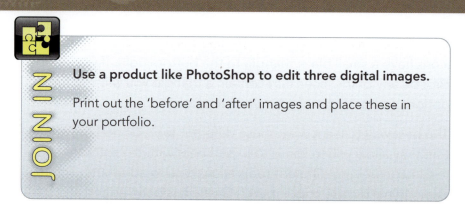

### Edit (working with DVD editing packages)

Just as you can use software like Adobe Photoshop to help you work with your photographs, software exists that helps you to work with and edit video clips. The video software used in the examples shown is Windows Movie Maker.

These example images were taken in Central Park, New York, after a heavy snow. Having imported the video clip or clips, you drag them onto the timeline at the base of the window. In the first image, nothing has been done to the clip.

FIGURE 6.17 New York video

The same video image has then been subjected to an editing effect called 3D Ripple (see Figure 6.18 on the next page). To apply the effect you literally drag and drop the effect onto the video segment in the timeline window (notice the addition of a star – this shows that an effect has been applied).

You will immediately see that buildings are bowed – the image is definitely different from the original. Having removed the first

FIGURE 6.18 New York video (3D Ripple)

chosen effect, we are now going to apply a second called Edge Detection. Again, we drag and drop the effect onto the video and the star reappears.

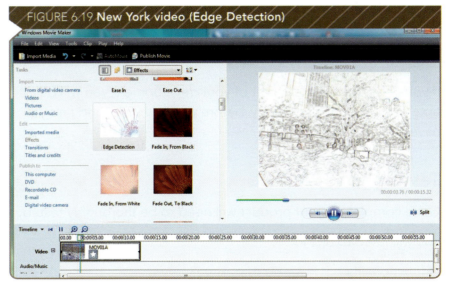

FIGURE 6.19 New York video (Edge Detection)

This is a very unusual effect because it turns the video into a line drawing. When the film is run, the whole sequence will appear in this form.

As with other software, it is always a good idea to experiment – although whilst you are learning to use the software, you might find it useful to write down what you did as you press buttons and apply effects.

### What are assets?

Your product's assets are all the different elements you have created that you will bring together in your final product. For example, you might have created some text, a sound file, a presentation and an edited DVD clip.

Repurposing your assets is essentially using these elements in different ways. You could, for example, crop some of the images or you could use software like Adobe Photoshop to change the colours of parts of the image.

When working with these different multimedia elements you have created, think about inventive ways you could use them!

### Your multimedia product

It is likely that your final product will be a combination of different assets.

### Prototyping

This is where you create your product asking the user as you are going along what he or she thinks about it. You will then need to respond to this feedback and make changes or adjustments as needed.

If you use prototyping as part of your development you will be able to make changes quickly, before you go too far and find you have a lot more to change.

## Testing your product

Once completed, your product will need to be thoroughly tested.

You will need to test for:

» functionality

» usability.

### Functionality

Remember the form you created before you designed your product, and the documentation you created to record your design plans? These documents will help you to identify what functions your product was supposed to have.

To test for functionality you will need to check that all the functions work as they were designed to. It usually helps to record this activity using a simple form like the one shown in Figure 6.20.

All you need to do is identify the functionality you will test, and how you will test it. You can then carry out the tests one by one and record in the last column exactly what happened when you did the test.

FIGURE 6.20 **Test log template**

| What functionality am I testing? | How will I test it? | What was the result when I tested it? |
|---|---|---|
| | | |
| | | |

An example of a completed test log can be seen in Figure 6.21.

FIGURE 6.21 **Completed test log**

| What functionality am I testing? | How will I test it? | What was the result when I tested it? |
|---|---|---|
| That the film runs when it is meant to. | Click on the button. | The film ran. |
| That the music plays as the user is shutting down the website. | Shut down the website. | The music did not play. This needs to be fixed! |
| The text can be easily read. | Ask someone else to read it. | The person was able to read the text. |

## Usability

Deciding whether the product is usable is usually done by asking others to test your product. To do this you need to give your testers instructions about what they need to do and then you should watch how they use your product. It is very helpful if you let them make comments about your product as they go through the instructions you have given.

If your users tell you that they have had any difficulties with your product, you will need to decide whether to fix these or whether to leave the product as it is, knowing that other users might experience the same problems but some might not.

### Fit for audience and purpose

On your original proposal form you were asked to identify the target users for your product.

One of the final activities in product development is deciding whether the final outcome or product met the original objectives. To make this decision you will need to consider the following.

» Does the product meet specified requirements?

» Does it include appropriate features?

» Is it suitable for the intended audience?

» Does it meet technical requirements?

**What do these mean?**

» *Does the product meet specified requirements?*
This means does the product do what it set out to do?

» *Does it include appropriate features?*
Does it have the right number of features or is there too much text, or too many pictures?

» *Is it suitable for the intended audience?*
Does the final product suit the audience it was intended for? Maybe it would help to look at a defined audience and think about the sorts of things this group expects in a product. (See Table 6.2).

» *Does it meet technical requirements?*
Is it in the right format to work with the existing system? An example of this could be that the product was created to work with Microsoft Windows and the user has got a different operating system such as Linux.

Is the file size appropriate? You might need to check that the computer the product will run on has enough free memory.

Is the screen resolution right? Don't forget that if the resolution of the user's screen is different from yours, the images might not look the same.

**TABLE 6.2 Is it suitable for the intended audience?**

| Audience | Definition and things to think about |
|---|---|
| Younger people | In this instance we will consider younger people to be anyone up to the age of 18.<br><br>• Young people like media products that are fun.<br>• They like them to be full of colour.<br>• They like them to be easy to navigate (move around).<br>• They like them to have interesting sounds or music.<br>• They like them to have lots of things to do.<br>• They don't like lots of text.<br>• Small children in particular like big buttons to click on.<br>• The language used will be simple, with more complex language used with teenagers.<br>• For the very young it is essential to use fewer words and to use large fonts. |

Having considered all these aspects you will be able to make a decision on the product's fitness for purpose.

# Be able to seek feedback from test users to identify opportunities for improvement

When your product is finished you will need to ask other people what they think of it. Ideally you should ask those in the target audience for their opinions, but you could also ask your classmates, family and friends.

## How can feedback be gathered?

It is better to gather feedback in a structured way than just to ask people what they think. This is because you will find it much easier to analyse information if everyone is asked the same questions. This in turn will enable you to make possible improvements for your product.

FIGURE 6.22 **Feedback form**

| Name (optional) | |
| Age | |
| Gender (M or F) | |
| Product | |

Please answer the following questions as honestly as you can (in each case circle your answer):

1. How easy was it to use the product?

   **Easy          OK          Hard          Very hard**

2. How appealing was the colour scheme?

   **Very appealing          OK          Horrible**

3. How good was the information provided?

   **Very good          OK          Not very good**

4. Would you use the product again?

   **Yes          No**

5. Please give any information about changes you would make:

   ...........................................................................

   ...........................................................................

   ...........................................................................

Thank you for completing this form!

## Questionnaire

Asking users to complete a questionnaire will give you a formal record that you can then use to make decisions. Prepare the questions carefully in advance.

## Interview

You could interview your users one by one – but in this case it would still be a good idea to have a list of questions to make sure that each person you interview is asked about the same things.

When it comes to designing the questionnaire/feedback form or the structure of the interview, similar considerations will apply as were applied to the product itself.

*Observation*

You could watch your users using the product and you could make notes, or you could observe them and then interview them afterwards.

*What is the feedback for?*

The feedback should allow you to find any errors. These are errors that were missed at testing – yes, this is possible! Any errors should be fixed as soon as possible. Sometimes the feedback will give you some ideas about how you could improve the product.

*What sorts of improvements could be made?*

If you ask for opinions, users are usually eager to tell you what they think about multimedia products. The usual criticisms that you will receive will depend on the type of product that was created.

Possible suggested improvements might include any or all of the following list, depending on which product you developed.

» Changing font size, making it bigger to make it easier to read, or smaller so that more text can be included.

» Images might need to be improved – they might not be very clear, or might be too large or too small.

» Users might suggest different colours or complain of combinations of colours that don't necessarily work very well together (for example, blue writing on a green background is difficult to read, particularly for colour-blind users).

» Users may spot inconsistencies in layout that need to be resolved.

» Sounds might not be clear or might not be audible (not loud enough).

When your product is finished and you have received feedback from a selection of users, you will be able to make judgements about what you could improve.

*Selecting your test users*

When selecting your product testers, make sure that they are representative of your target audience. It is no use selecting children to test a product made for adults, as it would probably be too difficult for them to use. So choose your test users very carefully.

# I want to be...

## ...a computer games designer

**Name:** Rick Goodman

**Age:** 32

### » Who do you work for?

I work in-house for a large software company that's based in Scotland, but some successful games designers work as consultants on a freelance basis. That's my ambition – to be able to pick and choose who I work for and when!

### » What do computer games designers do?

We do much more than just play games! We design the characters, plots and dialogue, create graphics in 2D and 3D, create game levels and sound effects, and check the game logic and playability. We leave the proper playing for the games testers who go through it afterwards, checking for bugs!

### » What skills do computer games designers need?

You need lots of creativity and imagination to bring someone else's ideas to life. It's unusual for us to create an entire game by ourselves, so you also need good communication skills and to be able to work as part of a large team. You also need good time management skills and, above all, good design skills!

Having said that, although you do need to be artistic and creative, you also need to have an appreciation of the technology so that you can design things that you know can actually be developed and will be playable without pushing the technology so far that it grinds to halt when people try to play the game.

### » What qualifications do games designers need?

Most of us have higher qualifications, such as a BTEC Higher National, a degree or a foundation degree. But you also need to gain experience wherever you can and build up a portfolio of your work. It's never too early to start thinking of ideas and writing them down!

### » What do you base your work on?

We usually work from a storyboard or an outline of the game that has already been created by the game's inventor. We then sit down with them and make sure that it's technically possible to do what they want us to do, before working together with the musical people, the graphics designers and everyone else to bring it all to life.

**✱ Rick Goodman**

# Case Study

## Website design →

The managers at Bandstuff.com feel that the company's website could be dramatically improved. In particular, they would like to make it more attractive to younger adults (those in the 14 to 18 age group).

## Questions

1 Discuss with your friends what they look for in a good website. From all the attributes identified, agree on five positive and five negative attributes and create a list, e.g.:

Positive attributes:
– Clear design
– Good range of colours
– Interesting images

Negative attributes:
– Too much text
– Not much to do

2 Ask each team member to find a different website and to evaluate it against the list. Each person then needs to identify two positive attributes that they feel MUST be incorporated in suggestions to improve the Bandstuff.com website.

3 Discuss your findings as a group and agree on four key attributes that you think make a contribution to a good website for an audience in the age range identified.

4 Create a brief PowerPoint presentation that explains these attributes and their importance to the managers at Bandstuff.com. Be prepared for your teacher/tutor to ask you to justify your choices and explain what you have learned from this exercise.

# Assessment Tips

For this unit you will need to present a portfolio which will be a combination of coursework assignments, classwork and activities. Your teacher/tutor will award marks across three mark bands for the work you have submitted.

## Task One: Investigate multimedia in business

You will be given an assignment that asks you to investigate two different uses of multimedia in business.

For each of the multimedia uses you will need to describe how and why multimedia is used.

## Task Two: Develop multimedia products

You will also be expected to design, develop, test and evaluate at least one, but ideally two or more, multimedia products.

You will need to have produced evidence of:

» Design
To do this you will have created design documentation for your products, providing enough detail that someone else could create the product based on your design.

» Development and testing
To do this you will have created and prepared digital assets and combined them to produce simple products, using prototyping and testing as part of the development process.

» Evaluation
After the products have been completed you will need to gather feedback from the test users to help you to identify ways in which your products could have been improved.

# SUMMARY / SKILLS CHECK

## » Design multimedia products

✓ You will have learned that in most cases products are developed within some constraints (limits) that you will either have set yourself or that will have been set for you by a client or a teacher/tutor. You will now have an appreciation of the range of documentation techniques you could use to focus your product, such as product ideas forms or storyboards.

## » Develop multimedia products

✓ Although the range of development opportunities in this book has been limited to graphics and video editing, you were free to use any software or media devices in the development of your products, as long as the final outcome met the criteria of the unit.

✓ You should always remember the eventual user in the development of your product and, if you are able to, you should ask the user for input as often as possible in the development of the product to make sure that you continue to meet the user's needs.

## » Test multimedia products

✓ Fully testing any developed product is absolutely essential because errors will need to be fixed quickly, otherwise they may make the product unusable.

✓ Through this unit you will have gained an understanding of simple testing techniques and recording mechanisms such as test logs. You will also understand that involving your user or users in this process is vital.

✓ Using techniques such as questionnaires, interviews and observations will allow you to gain feedback that can also be used in the final evaluation of your product.

## » Evaluate products

✓ Everyone would agree that evaluation is an important tool in helping to learn. Clearly, if you evaluate a product, you can learn from your mistakes. You should be able to identify whether the mistakes were made during the design process or during implementation.

✓ Sometimes the error was made even before design began, if the product needed was not identified properly! Learning where errors have been made will ensure that you do not make the same mistakes again.

# Glossary

**animation**   a moving image created through drawings – like a cartoon.

**anti-spyware**   software which can detect and remove *Spyware*.

**anti-virus**   *software* that detects, repairs or deletes files infected with a computer *virus*.

**application**   *software* designed to fit the specific needs of a user by performing a particular task.

**autoNumber**   a data type used in *database* design to identify each record in a *database* table. The autoNumber increases automatically as each record is created.

**back-up**   a copy of important data that is stored somewhere else.

**bit**   the smallest unit of data possible in an IT system.

**broadband**   a computer connection (to the outside world). Usually described in terms of its bandwidth, which is the speed at which it is able to transfer data. Broadband is usually 1024 kbps or faster.

**byte**   8 *bits* together.

**CD (compact disc)**   a *device* for storing digital files – both data files and music files. CDs come in two types – writable and rewritable. The content of a writable CD cannot be changed once data has been stored to it.

**database**   a file created using a piece of *software*. The file contains organisational records and other information in a logical way so that the data can be used.

**device**   a machine or component developed to attach to a computer, or which is based on computer technology. A printer is an example of a device that attaches to a computer. An iPod is a device that attaches to a computer, but can also be used in isolation once the files have been uploaded to it.

**drive**   a *device* used for reading and writing disks, or other components, that store data. For example, a *DVD* drive reads and writes DVDs.

**DVD (Digital Versatile Disc)**   a device for storing electronic files. DVDs can store much more data than *CD*s.

**emoticon**   a facial expression produced by a series of key presses. For example, : and ) typed one after the other produce a :) (smiley).

**EPOS (Electronic Point Of Sale system)**   a type of system found in shops. EPOS processes stock transactions and sales.

**Ethernet cable**   a type of cable that connects devices.

**field**   a column in a *database* used to group data items. For example, a date of birth field in a database holds all records of dates of birth in a single column.

**firewall**   *hardware* or *software* that filters network traffic to prevent unauthorised access, but allows outward messages to be sent.

**gigabyte**   the largest unit of data storage.

**graphic**   the term used to describe all images – including pictures, charts and graphs.

**graphics card**   a component that generates video image, which is displayed on the computer monitor.

**hard disk**   a component inside the computer that stores the *operating system*, *applications software* and files.

**hardware**   anything in a computer system that you can touch. For example, the monitor, casing, *modem* and mouse.

**heatsink and fan**   components that work together to draw heat away from the computer's processor.

**input**   something the user introduces to an *application*; for example, a name and address.

**installation**   the act of putting together a computer system – uploading the operating system and *applications* software and connecting and configuring *devices*.

**Internet**   millions of *websites* connected together used by individuals or organisations to communicate and share information.

**intranet**   a private network created for use within an organisation that uses *Internet* technology. It can be accessed only by people within the organisation.

**ISP (Internet Service Provider)**   a business that provides access to the Internet.

**keyboard**   a *device* used to enter text and numbers.

**kilobyte**   1024 *bytes*.

**LAN (Local Area Network)**   a group of computers linked together over a short distance.

**LCD (Liquid Crystal Display)**   the technology behind newer display monitors.

**megabyte**   1024 *kilobytes*.

**modem**   a network device that connects a *Local Area Network (LAN)* to the *ISP's (Internet Service Provider)* servers, and then to the *Internet*.

**motherboard**   the main component of an IT system. All the other components are connected to the motherboard.

**narrowband**   a computer connection (to the outside world). Usually described in terms of its bandwidth, which is the speed at which it is able to transfer data. Narrowband is about 56kbps.

**network address**   a unique address for each network *device* used by the control systems to identify different network machines.

**network card**   a *device* that plugs into the *motherboard* and can send and receive network data.

**operating system**   controls the *hardware* and supports the running of *applications*.

**output**   something produced by a computer system, such as a printed document or a view on a monitor.

**PDA (Personal Digital Assistant)**   a hand-held *device* that is effectively a mini computer. It usually runs versions of standard programs with limited functionality.

**peer-to-peer**   a minimum of two fully-working systems that are connected together.

**pixel**   small dots of colour that form an image.

**primary key/unique identifier**   a piece of data in a record that is unique and will not be used in another record.

**processor**   the "brain" of an IT system that performs all the calculations that are required. Also called the central processing unit (CPU).

**query**   a *database* tool that extracts records depending on the criteria requested.

**RAM (Random Access Memory)**   temporary storage of data in the IT system while it is being processed.

**report (Database)**   a formal output from a *database* containing a heading or headings and page numbers.

**report (Document)**   a formal multi-page document used by organisations to record information around particular issues.

**resolution**   the number of *pixels* on a monitor or flat panel.

**router**   a network *device*, often wireless, that handles connections between different networks; directing network traffic to the correct destination.

**server**   A server is a bit like a master computer that manages a specific resource or set of resources (like a network).

**SMS (Short Message Service)**   computerised service for sending text messages to a mobile phone.

**software**   a general term for *applications* or programs designed to carry out specific tasks.

**sort**   a method of organising data in a predicted way. For example from A to Z for text, or 1 to 100 for numbers.

**sound card**   a *device* that generates the sound effects and music heard through speakers or headphones.

**spreadsheet**   a computer program used when working with numbers.

**spyware**   software that enables a user to gain data and send data to another's computer without their knowledge.

**storyboard**   a series of images used in film work, *animation* and computer programming to represent what a computer-related product will look like.

**switch or hub**   an electronic *device* that shares network communication with connected devices.

**table**   a grid in a *database* that contains a series of records.

**validation**   a mechanism added by the developer to a *database* field to make sure that the data input into a field is correct.

**virus**   a mini program introduced intentionally, but secretly, to a computer system to damage it. Each virus type does something different, from simply hiding files or directories to deleting them.

**WAN (Wide Area Network)**   a group of computers linked together over a large distance.

**web browser**   a software *application* used to view web pages from the *Internet*.

**web page**   an electronic document, usually containing text and graphics, that is accessed via a viewer called a *web browser*.

**webcam**   a mini camera that sends a live image.

**website**   collections of related *web pages* created to be used together.

**wireless**   technology that connects *devices* without cables. Wireless is popular, but less secure than wired systems. Signals can be weakened by distance and interference.

**workstation**   a term used to describe a computer linked to a network so that the user can access the network's resources.

# Index

We are grateful to the following for permission to reproduce copyright material:

The AA for 2 screenshots adapted from www.theaa.com, reproduced with permission; Adobe Systems Incorporated for Adobe Photoshop® product screen shots reprinted with permission from Adobe Systems Incorporated; AVG for a screenshot from http://free.avg.com, reproduced with permission; Cadbury for a still image from a Cadbury television advertisement, reproduced with permission; Cineworld for 4 screenshots from www.cineworld.co.uk, reproduced with permission; Concurrent Design Group for a screenshot from www.printin3d.co.uk copyright © CDG, reproduced with permission; EarthCam, Inc for a screenshot from www.earthcam.com, reproduced courtesy of EarthCam, Inc.; eBay International A.G. for a screenshot from http://www.ebay.co.uk, reproduced with permission of eBay Inc. copyright © Ebay Inc. All rights reserved; Edexcel Limited for a screenshot from www.edexcel.org.uk, reproduced with permission; FreeOnlineSurveys.com for a screenshot from www.FreeOnlineSurveys.com, reproduced with permission; Google for a screenshot from www.google.co.uk, reproduced with permission; Kernowcraft Rocks & Gems Ltd for a screenshot from www.kernowcraft.com, copyright © Kernowcraft, reproduced with permission; Lila-SE for a screenshot from www.lila-se.de, reproduced with permission; Microsoft for Microsoft product screen shots, reprinted with permission from Microsoft Corporation; Moodle.com for a screenshot from www.moodle.org; reproduced with permission; Mozilla Europe for a screenshot of Mozilla Firefox www.mozilla.com/en-US copyright © Mozilla Europe, reproduced with permission; Napster for a screenshot from www.napster.co.uk, reproduced with permission; Pearson Education Limited for a screenshot from www.pearson.com, reproduced with permission; Purbeck District Council for a screenshot from www.purbeck.gov.uk, reproduced with permission; Royal Mail for a screenshot from http://track.royalmail.com, reproduced with permission; Scholastic Inc. for a screenshot from www.teacher/Scholastic.com reproduced with permission; Skype for a Skype SMS screenshot, reproduced with permission; Transport for London for a screenshot from www.cclondon.com, reproduced with permission; and Uretopia Limited for a screenshot from www.myhotspots.co.uk, reproduced with permission.